OPEN LOOK

Canadian Basketball and Me

JAY TRIANO

with Michael Grange

Published by Simon & Schuster

New York   London   Toronto   Sydney   New Delhi

In basketball and in life, to get an open look, you need the strategy of a coach, and the assist or help from a teammate.

To all the coaches, players, and teammates I have encountered through the game of basketball, thanks for the open look.

CONTENTS

OPEN LOOK

PROLOGUE

Coach Donohue had rules. They were unwritten, but we all knew them. He had rules about being clean shaven: "You need to stand closer to the mirror next time," he'd say if we showed up with too much stubble. He had rules about taking our hats off when we came inside, about making sure we didn't stay out in the sun for longer than thirty minutes, and about not chewing gum in public. "It makes you look like a cow," he'd say in his native Brooklynese.

But the number one unwritten rule was that the first seat on the bus was his.

I played basketball for Jack Donohue on the Canadian national team for eleven years. We travelled all over the world. We had our hearts broken many times. We laughed a thousand times more. And once, my teammates and I lifted Jack onto our shoulders to cut down the nets after dreaming the impossible dream and fighting the impossible foe—Jack's favourite line from his favourite musical, *Man of La Mancha*. We had dreamed of beating Team USA, and we'd finally done it on our way to a gold medal in the 1983 World University Games. On home court, no less.

I was a kid the day I celebrated with Jack on my shoulders. We all were. With a head full of long, dark hair, I had the whole world ahead of me.

Thirty-two years later, in 2015, I was sitting on a bus in Mexico City, thinking back to that earlier version of myself. I wasn't a kid anymore; I was a man, a father of three grown children. What hair I had was shaved short and as grey as Jack's had been. And I'd taken the torch that Jack had passed; I was the head coach of the Canadian men's national team.

I was clean shaven, I wasn't chewing gum, and I was in the first seat on the bus. Jack's seat. Behind me on our charter was the most talented basketball team Canada had ever assembled. There were eight NBA players on our twelve-man roster; six had been first-round picks, two of whom had been taken first overall.

As it so often did, our whole summer—the next four years, in some ways—came down to one game. If we won our semifinal against Venezuela that day, we would qualify for the 2016 Olympic Games in Rio de Janeiro. There was a time—when Jack was the head coach and I was a player—when Canada had been a fixture in Olympic basketball. But since Jack had retired in 1988, Canada had been to just one Olympics. It was time to get us back to where we'd been and help these players achieve something real and pure, something that they'd never forget.

Jack's teams had never been this talented, but we'd been true teams, savvy and tough. All that bad food and those long flights and battles when we felt as though we were alone in a foreign place fighting for one another—sometimes literally—had created a bond that lived deep in our bones. I wanted the same thing for the guys on the bus with me. My goal was to win, to do something on the international stage that no Canadian team before had pulled off: to stand on the winners' podium at an Olympic Games or a World Championship.

But to do that, we would have to beat Venezuela.

As the bus wound through traffic, the players had their headphones on, staring out the window at the city of 21 million, all of whom seemed to be on the road at the same time. Some of the guys were nodding to music I wouldn't recognize. Others were scrolling through their phones, catching up on news back home. The rest of our staff and I made small talk, but there wasn't much to say. Our work was done. We'd had our meetings, gone over our video, installed our game plan. That's the worst part of game day: the wait.

Jack's message on the eve of a big game—and in international basketball, every game is a big one—was to treat every game the same. Prepare the same way, adhere to your routines, trust your habits. Make something too big, and you'd send the wrong signals to your players. Take an opponent too lightly, and you'd pay the price.

In the locker room before the game, I tried to channel Jack.

"You know the stakes," I said to the team. "Win and we're in. Venezuela is tough, we know that. Let's get a foot in the door, and then we'll break it down."

The game was a battle right from the tip. The Venezuelans were holding and grabbing, and the calls weren't coming. Cory Joseph, our heart-and-soul point guard, was getting the treatment.

The Venezuelans double-teamed him, and he was getting banged around. That was a bigger problem than usual because Nik Stauskas, one of our best ball handlers, was beside me on the bench. Two nights before, he'd eaten a burrito from a street vendor. He'd spent the next day and night in hospital, hooked up to an IV. He had tried to play, but after two days without food, he had nothing to give.

Venezuela was in control of the tempo. As the first half was winding down, one of its guards hit a pull-up, fading three at the buzzer with Cory draped all over him. The shot gave Venezuela a one-point lead heading into the half. In the second half, things picked up right where they'd left off, as we battled for every inch up and down the court.

As the fourth quarter wound down, it finally felt as though we were in control. With just over three minutes to play, we were up seven points. But then Venezuela hit another three at the end of the shot clock to cut the lead to four. We traded misses, and then Venezuela came back another three. Our lead was almost gone with sixty-nine seconds left. Kelly Olynyk—as skilled a big man as Canada has ever had—brought the ball up to relieve some pressure on Cory. But as he stepped on the logo at centre court, his foot slipped out from under him. We should have seen it coming—players had been sliding on the logo for the whole tournament. Olynyk lost the ball and reached up to foul the Venezuelan defender to prevent a fast break. They made both free throws, and, just like that, the Venezuelans were up by a point with barely a minute to play.

The Mexican crowd, hoping to play Venezuela in the final, started cheering against us—chants of "Vene-zuela, Vene-zuela" rang through the stadium. I called a time-out and drew up a play for Andrew Wiggins to get the ball to Andrew Nicholson in the post.

Wiggins made a smart read after the inbound, driving to the basket and dishing instead to Olynyk, who scored. We were back up with fifty seconds to go, but Venezuela wasn't done yet. They scored on a layup to take a one-point lead. On our next possession, Nicholson was fouled and given two free throws. He missed his first but made the second, and we were tied with twenty-four seconds to play.

Coaching is about thinking of a dozen different things at once. You're trying to solve problems, but with each advancing second, the equations are changing. When do you use your time-outs? When do you call in your substitutions? Are the best free-throw shooters on the floor? If so, will I be able to get our best defensive group out when I need them? What are the matchups, and whom should we attack? It all happens fast. Preparation is critical, but sometimes in such moments, the best thing you can do has nothing to do with what's happening on the court but what is going on inside the players' heads. You simply have to make sure your players are calm; remind them to breathe and focus on the next play, leaving what just happened behind. A veteran team makes things simpler. They've been in these moments before; they've been in them together. They know how to walk through the fire.

This time, though, we got burned. Venezuela had the ball. We had our best defensive lineup on the floor and our best rebounders. We expected them to put up a late shot, leaving just enough time to have a chance at a put-back but not enough for us to score from our end of the floor.

We guessed right. Our defence was great, and Venezuela's shot drew iron. The rebound went straight up off the rim. As I watched the ball hang in the air, for a split second I felt relief. *Looks like we're going to overtime*, I thought. With that ball suspended, I was ready to bet everything that we were going to the Olympics. But then reality came crashing back. There was a scrum, bodies were flying. Then a whistle. The foul was on us.

In my fifth decade of international basketball, I felt I'd seen everything. But this was something else—a loose-ball foul with a fraction of a second on the clock. Venezuela had two free throws with 0.3 second left. Not far from our bench, a group of reporters from Venezuela were losing their minds—they couldn't believe what was happening, either.

The first free throw went in to put Venezuela up one. The shooter intentionally missed the second so that the clock ran out, robbing us of whatever sliver of a chance we had for a desperation heave. The final buzzer sounded, and it was over. We'd lost. We weren't going to the Olympics.

The mood in the dressing room afterward was tense. I looked around at the young players, a mixture of anger and heartbreak painted across all of their faces. I felt for them; I'd been in the same situation more than once.

I thought about what Jack would have done. So many of my seasons under Jack had ended just short of the ultimate goal. Almost all of them, really. Only one gold medal is given out; only one team ends its year with the ultimate victory. Each time, though, Jack would thank us for our time and our commitment. He'd encourage us to learn and grow from the disappointment, telling us that we'd be better for it. Once again Jack was with me as I turned to address the guys in the room.

"You guys fought hard out there," I told the team. "I'm proud of each and every one of you. I can't make this feel any better right now, but I want you to know—this isn't the end, it's a beginning.

You're young, and this is one of those hard lessons you have to learn. Don't let this stop you. The best is yet to come."

I'm not sure my guys wanted to hear it any more than I had when I played. But like so many wise words you hear when you're young, they truly make sense only when you're the one giving the message.

Jack knew, better than anyone else, that when you really love something, there are times—a lot of times—when your journey is going to hurt, and it's going to leave a mark. But that doesn't mean you stop dreaming big dreams. Jack taught me that, and I've never stopped.

CHAPTER 1

DREAMING BIG DREAMS

I grew up in Tillsonburg, Ontario, about a hundred miles west of Niagara Falls and a two-hour drive from Toronto. Strangely enough, in my early years, Tillsonburg might have been the centre of basketball in Canada. The sport was still several decades away from becoming part of Canada's urban fabric, a change that would alter the trajectory of the sport in our country. Back then, though, basketball was kind of a hit-and-miss thing. In some communities, there were dedicated coaches and leaders, and the sport was embraced. In other communities, the legacy sports of hockey and lacrosse still reigned supreme.

Tillsonburg was one of those places where basketball had taken root, mainly because of Gerry Livingston. Gerry was a big dreamer, a basketball fanatic, and a local legend. He started a business manufacturing wooden shipping crates and wooden parts for automobiles and farm implements in 1941 in London, Ontario, and later moved it to Tillsonburg as it grew. It became quite a business, but he was one of those guys who wanted to do more than just make his money and move on. He believed in building a community and making people proud of it. One way he did that was to use his business to sponsor sports teams. He founded a senior men's basketball team, the Tillsonburg Livingstons, that won the 1959 Canadian senior men's national championship and earned the right to represent Canada at the Pan American Games in Chicago in 1959. It was another accomplishment in the Livvies' storied history—in 1952, the team had won the Canadian senior men's national championship and with it the right to represent Canada at the Olympics in Helsinki that year. The original backbone of that team was Bill Coulthard, who lived in the neighborhood, across from the high school, and had a hoop in front of his house.

I was too young and small to shoot on the Coulthards' basket, but there were always neighbourhood kids playing on it. As soon as I heard the ball hitting the driveway and the other kids shouting to start a game, I would go tearing out the door and down the street. I'd sit on the Coulthards' lawn and watch the older kids shoot around. Bill Coulthard's sons all ended up being excellent players, and the youngest, David, went on to become one of the greatest players in Canadian university basketball history, an unbelievable shooter who was a five-time all-Canadian and twice won the Mike Moser award as Canada's player of the year, before being drafted by the Detroit Pistons in 1982.

That spirit of play—just doing what was in front of you and what was fun in the moment—was a big part of my experience growing up. I was competitive, as were my sister, Jody, and my brother, Jeff.

When Jeff was old enough, the two of us would often battle head-to-head, but my love of sports started because it was fun.

We could turn anything into a game, and we used whatever we had. We played one-on-one baseball or two-on-two—we didn't wait around until there were nine guys and a coach to tell us what to do. The gymnasium at my junior school faced our backyard, and the wall of the gym was two or three stories tall—like the Green Monster at Fenway. My brother and I would throw a hard-ball up and hit it from our backyard toward the wall of the gym. If it went onto the roof, it was an automatic end of game—you lost, and you had to climb up on the roof to get the ball back. If the ball hit the wall a certain distance up without going over, it was a home run. If it hit the wall below that line, it was a triple, and one bounce and to the wall was a double, with singles being anything past the pitcher that made it to the wall on more than one bounce. So one guy was in the field and the other guy was out there just swinging the shit out of the ball until you were both too tired to go on.

The first organized basketball I played took place in a church league run out of Lundy's Lane United Church in Niagara Falls, where we moved when I was five or six years old. Most of our coaches were just kids from nearby Stamford Collegiate. In one of my earliest games, I was called for travelling. I didn't understand what the problem was—I was walking up the floor with the ball tucked under my arm, imitating my coach during our practices. After the ref blew his whistle, I looked over at my coach in confusion.

"What are you doing?" he asked. "Did you think there was a time-out or something?"

"Oh, yeah." I realized what I had done and made sure to dribble the next time I got the ball.

As much as basketball was part of my earliest memories, it wasn't until I was in high school that it became important to me to the exclusion of other sports. I played baseball growing up every summer—I was a slap-hitting first baseman with good speed on a team that won the national championship in 1974. But when I reached high school, I was almost six foot three and pretty skinny, so I wasn't hitting with a lot of power. I'd make contact, and if the fielder bobbled it I had a pretty good chance of getting on base. But it was clear that baseball was going to be just a casual summertime thing for me. We had some great players on that team, and I was far from a star. It would have been easy to get frustrated and just turn away from the team and the sport, blaming them for my struggles or for not giving me a chance. But I'd learned that every situation—good or bad—can teach you something, and I give my parents credit for that.

The year our team won the national midget baseball championship, I didn't play a whole lot—I was a better teammate than player early on, and I was younger than most of the other guys on the team. But I always tried to stay positive. I was constantly talking to the guys on the bench and cheering them on. It helped to keep me in the game; when my chance came to step in, I didn't want to let my teammates down.

At the year-end banquet, our coach was giving out the awards for the year, and when it came time for the best teammate award, he started by describing the meaning of the recognition.

"This player has showed us that everybody has a role on the team," he began. "It's not your stat line or your highlight reel that matters. It's who you are as a person and how you treat the people around you. This player represented all of the best qualities of an athlete."

Halfway through my coach's speech, one of my teammates nudged me, and it dawned on me—our coach was talking about me. The next thing I knew, people were clapping and someone was slapping me on the back and telling me to go to the stage. I was stunned. I hadn't even known the team gave out that award, and I felt a wave of emotions churning inside me. As I walked to the front of the room, I struggled to keep from crying from gratitude. *Not in front of the older guys*, I thought. As I shook my coach's hand, I realized that being a good teammate was a transferable skill—a lesson I still tell players today.

It's hard for me to imagine what it would have been like growing up somewhere else in Ontario or Canada. Would I have had the same love of sports? Would I have done something entirely different with my life? I'm happy that I did grow up there, but I think that border towns are a little bit different, especially back then. When I was a kid, there was obviously no Internet, and even television coverage was a fraction of what we have today. But living on the Niagara River, I had the benefit of TV, radio, and every other bit of media coming from the United States. I could go to both Niagara University and Buffalo Braves games—they were just a quick trip across the border, no big deal. I'm Canadian, but I'm a Canadian by only fifty yards.

When you live in a small community like that, a community that is invested in sport, it's a unique environment because your role models are so accessible. Gordon Singleton was a track cyclist from Niagara Falls, just a couple of years older than me, and when he went to the Olympics in Montreal in 1976 at just nineteen years old, it blew me away. The infrastructure of sports was built into our daily lives, whether it was the *Friday Night Lights* feel of basketball and baseball games in the summer or the Niagara Falls Flyers, our Junior A hockey team. My grandmother boarded a few players for the local junior hockey team. I loved visiting her house when the players were there so that I could soak in the atmosphere and listen to them talk about sports. My favourite player was Steve Atkinson. Sometimes before a game, I would walk over from my grandmother's house with him so that he could sneak me into the arena.

Successful people come from all kinds of communities, but I do sometimes wonder if there is a sweet spot—a place big enough that there is some competition and opportunity but small enough that people know and look out for one another while at the same time making sure that people with talent and drive can be identified, supported, and pushed on.

I found some of that success in other sports. I played volleyball in high school, and I was a good enough high jumper that I made it to the OFSAA, the provincial high school championships. But I always kept coming back to basketball. I mean, high jump is fun, but how many times do you get to jump at a track meet? And it's not as though you're going to get together with your buddies and do some high jumping on a Saturday. But basketball? There was something about it that appealed to me as a kid and that still appeals to the kid in me today. What caught me at first was watching the ball go through the hoop. Every time I saw the ball drop through the net, I felt a sense of accomplishment—it was an unequivocal sign that I'd done something right. I wanted to do it over and over again.

When I was in high school, I finally got my own basketball hoop at home. As soon as the hoop was in place, I was out there constantly. Our neighbours, Enzo and Rita Felassete, would often complain about the noise my dribbling made: "Jay, it's eleven o'clock. Please go to bed." That driveway court was my release, the place where I could just go and shoot the ball and let the rest of the world fall away. To this day, when I shoot the ball, there's nothing else in that moment other than me, the ball, and the hoop. Success seeing it go through. That's where the fun starts—trying to make shots. Then you start having a little bit of success, and it's even more fun.

Our driveway was cement, so it had seams so that it wouldn't crack. I would go to each spot, and I'd be a different NBA player, and I'd have to shoot 1-2-3-4-5-6-7 shots. I would be Randy Smith, and then I'd be John Havlicek. I'd build tournaments and playoff brackets, and I would play teams against one another, with me being the star player of each team. I even kept track of each tournament on the wall inside the garage door. And when I did it, ironically enough, I would broadcast the game, calling the plays as I went—part of my early training, I guess.

"Ernie D brings it over the timeline, swings it to Randy Smith. McAdoo sets a screen. Smith drives and misses!" I'd yell as my shot bounced off the rim. "But he picks up the rebound and pitches out to McAdoo, who lays it back in."

If I missed a shot, it was the other team's ball, and if I made it, I'd keep shooting for that team. Without knowing it, I was using visualization. Today, that's a big part of performance improvement—being able to powerfully visualize yourself playing well and having success. But I didn't know that at the time; I was just pump faking John Havlicek in my driveway. I'd drive to the net, pump fake, and imagine him flying by as I ducked underneath his block.

My makeshift practices served me well when we went away for school tournaments. It was a huge deal for us to play at Oakwood Collegiate Institute in downtown Toronto. It had a good team, so we were always excited to make the trip down from the Falls to the city. The first time we drove there, I remember how much we hyped up the game. But when we got to the school, we couldn't believe how small the gym was. It turned out that most schools in the heart of the city had small gyms—due to lack of space. Oakwood knew how to use the gym size to its advantage, and they ran super-aggressive, full-court-press defences. It should have intimidated me, but my first thought was just *This gym is tiny. I'll bet I can shoot from centre.* So I did. I took a shot from centre and made it. The other team couldn't believe it.

That wasn't the most memorable part of the trip, though. Partway through the game, I was elbowed above my eye. My forehead immediately split open, and I was bleeding a lot. We were able to stop the bleeding so that I could keep playing, but after the game, the cut was still open and oozing. I didn't care, though, because I had bigger priorities: I had a dance to get back to at school! We roared back in time for the dance, and when it finally wrapped up, I told my friends, "I've got to go to the hospital now." My parents met me there, and they were livid. "What were you thinking? First of all, you should have gone to straight to the hospital. You don't drive back, and then you definitely don't go to a dance." I didn't understand why my parents were so upset. The doctor had been able to patch me up, and it was a school dance—no way I could miss that! Some things were more important than basketball, or so I thought.

That changed, though, and slowly but surely, basketball began to take over my life. In high school, I didn't love math, but I had to do a project on statistics, so I decided to do it on basketball. I had a big poster of Wilt Chamberlain dunking on the wall of my room, and I presented my data on Chamberlain's recent season. It was the first time I'd been excited about a math project, and it must have shown, because the teacher put my stats up on the wall in class.

At a certain point, being a basketball player started to become more of an identity, not just a sport I played but a way I thought about myself. When you're a kid, all your dreams are big dreams. As you get older, they become more specific, but you need examples to make it concrete—people or things that get you excited about what is possible. They don't have to be big things. In 1976, after the Olympics in Montreal, my family collected some Olympic posters, which we had framed and hung on the stairway going down to our rec room. I must have passed those posters thousands of times going up and down our stairs, and every time I did, it built up my dreams and my pride in Canada a little more.

The Buffalo Braves were the first professional basketball team I ever saw live, but funnily enough, I first saw them in Toronto at Maple Leaf Gardens, where they were facing "Pistol Pete" Maravich and the Atlanta Hawks. The Braves played ten games a year in Toronto. The older guys from my high school senior team decided to drive up, and even though I was only in grade ten, they took me with them. Maravich wore number 44, and he was electric—I couldn't take my eyes off of him. He was a skinny, six-foot-five white guy who had so much flair and style. He was dominant—he had led the NBA in scoring—but critics said he wasn't passing the ball enough, and so the next year, he led the NBA in assists. I felt as though I were watching my future. I was a six-foot-five white kid, and I thought, *I can be that guy. This is it. This is who I can be.*

All of a sudden I had a picture in my mind's eye of what a really, really good basketball player could look like, and I tried to match that picture. When I went home, I cut the elastics out of all my socks so that I could have the same droopy socks as Maravich. I got hold of his book, and I never put it down. His father, Peter "Press" Maravich, had been a coach, which made me feel like I could relate to Pete even more. Maravich was famous for taking a basketball with him everywhere he went, so from that point on, I did the same. I took it to school with me. If my friends went to see a movie, I took my ball to the theatre. You know when you graduate from high school and everyone signs your yearbook? I got my basketball signed. It's completely smooth; there's not a pebble on it because I dribbled the thing everywhere I went.

It's hard to pinpoint how you end up on a certain path in life. I can't say that all those hours shooting on my driveway, making up games to keep myself amused, led to me playing on the national team. But if there was a constant when I was growing up, it was basketball and the fun and enjoyment it provided me. When you find something like that at a young age, you don't turn your back on it. You keep gravitating to it. And luckily for me, basketball had only just begun to pull me into its orbit.

CHAPTER 2

LEARNING FROM TERRY

You never know where life will take you before you get there. Basketball was obviously a big thing in our house growing up. But it wasn't the only thing. My brother's passion was hockey, and my sister swam and played softball. We each had dreams, and we each found our path toward them.

My dreams didn't start in the bright lights of any big city, though. My path had a modest beginning. As we lived close to the United States, it wasn't uncommon for us to head across the border to catch basketball games, especially with the Buffalo Braves of the NBA playing so close. And Niagara University, a tiny Catholic school in Lewiston, New York, was an unlikely basketball powerhouse in the late 1960s and 1970s under the guidance of Frank Layden, who later went on to become a renowned NBA coach.

But on that occasion at Niagara's Gallagher Center, I wasn't going to watch the Purple Eagles. Instead, I was there to see the Red and White.

It was my first time watching the Canadian national team play. They were gearing up for the 1976 Olympics in Montreal, so they were playing exhibition games wherever they could find them. I was looking forward to watching the game, the same way I looked forward to any live basketball game I went to. But I didn't have any sense of the occasion or what it represented.

When I entered the arena, though, I was blown away. The atmosphere was crazy. A small contingent of Canadians had come out to support the national team; most of them were students at Niagara, some of whom were there to cheer on the American college team. But the intimate crowd was what made it special. International hockey had just started to take off in the 1970s—I watched the final game of the Summit Series against the Soviet Union in my grade school class like everyone else my age, and I went crazy when Paul Henderson scored—and it seemed that the same excitement was carrying into the basketball world.

Seeing that play out on a basketball court touched something inside me. The Canadian team was the underdog, but they fought so hard. I felt the hair on the back of my neck stand up when I realized that those guys were competing for something so much bigger than a team or even friendship. A light went on. As a kid, I didn't have a lot of readily accessible or realistic basketball models to follow for success. It wasn't as though there were NBA games being broadcast every time I turned on the TV, and there definitely weren't dozens of Canadian guys in the league whom I could follow. Even if I did get a chance to see a professional team like the Braves once in a while, it didn't feel real. The players were all American guys from places I didn't know or had only heard about. How could I watch Bob McAdoo, a Buffalo Braves star and future NBA Hall of Famer, and think, *I'm going to be just like him one day.*

But watching the national team? That was different. Those guys looked like me and came from places I knew. It seemed accessible. The setting was modest—the gym at Niagara University looked and felt like every other small university gym that I'd been to, able to fit in only a few thousand people at most. But the game suddenly felt epic.

After the game, most of the students filed off, but I stayed in my seat as the national anthems played. The small group of Canadians around me all stood and broke into "O Canada" as the music played. I looked down to the court and saw all of the players staring proudly up at our flag in the rafters. Suddenly it hit me: *That's what I want to do. I want to play for the national team.*

The next day, I was back at school, telling anyone who would listen to me about the game, including my coaches at A.N. Myer Secondary School.

"I have a plan," I told my senior coach, Paul Deeton. "Graduate, go to Simon Fraser University, make the national team, play in the Olympics."

Mr. Deeton was always really positive with me, but after I told him my plan, he looked at me like I had two heads. "Jay," he said, "you've got to be realistic."

"What is there to be realistic about?" I asked. "I'm going to win a gold medal for Canada. How complicated could it be?"

Mr. Deeton took me down to the library and pulled out my student record. He pointed to my—admittedly very average—marks.

"Jay, you can't play for the Canadian national team if you don't get into university. How are you going to get into Simon Fraser with these grades?"

It was a bit of a comedown, obviously. I had always been an average student. If I was interested in a topic, I'd work hard and do well enough. But I wasn't all that interested all that often, and my grades reflected that. How can you do homework when there's always another basketball game to play or baseball practice or the guys in the neighbourhood are playing touch football or ball hockey—you get the picture.

Mr. Deeton's question snapped me to attention. It was the first time I started looking ahead and getting excited about a big, specific goal after high school. I made the connection that what I was doing in high school—basketball aside—actually mattered in the context of those goals. Better late than never, I guess. Besides, I'm sure Coach Deeton knew exactly what he was doing when he pulled out my report card. When you tell me I can't do something—that I can't be a student, can't play—I don't get discouraged; I get motivated to prove people wrong.

So I started putting in the work, and my grades picked up. In my last year in high school, everyone knew that it was SFU or bust for me—I didn't have a backup plan.

Having basketball coaches as teachers didn't hurt. My grade nine coach, Peter Higgins, was also my grade thirteen chemistry teacher. One day I was sitting in class, and Mr. Higgins asked, "Jay, what do you need to get into university?"

"I need a seventy-seven in this class, sir."

Mr. Higgins paused for a moment. "Okay, if you keep doing your work, I'll give it to you."

The class immediately erupted into protest. "You can't
one girl yelled. "I'm trying to get into university, too!"

"You do the work, and I'll decide the marks," Mr. Higgi
plied. He was joking, but I have to thank those guys for recogn
what was important to me and motivating me to get there.

The hard work paid off, and in the spring of 1977, Stan Stewai
son, the head coach at Simon Fraser University, visited me at hom
to recruit me. He didn't have to work very hard. We sat in the living
room, my parents on either side of me on the couch, facing Stan
across from us.

"We have an intense schedule, Jay. We head down to the States
regularly to play NAIA teams, even some Division Ones, too. We
might even be heading out to Hawaii next year for a tournament."

"That sounds amazing!" I said.

"We're also pleased to offer you a scholarship."

"Yes," I said. "I'm in."

Stan paused. "Sorry, don't you want to hear all of the details?"
he asked.

I looked at my parents, and my mom said, "Show him why."

I ran up to my room and grabbed the program from the Canadian national team game at Niagara University, which had been
sitting beside my bed for two years. I bounded back down the stairs
and handed the program to Stan.

"Billy Robinson, Alex Devlin, Tom Skerlak—I want to be like
those guys. I want to play for Team Canada. I want to wear the red
and white. If SFU was good enough for those guys, that's where I
want to be."

Stan was as sold as I was. I signed there and then, and we

arranged for me to go visit the school later in the summer. When I set foot on the campus grounds, I knew I'd made the right decision. The SFU campus is on top of Burnaby Mountain, and though it's just a thirty-minute drive from downtown Vancouver, the city could be three hours away. The campus feels as though it's in a national park—it sits above everything else on the crest of the mountain, two thousand feet in the air, with nothing but trees between you and the city below. I later learned that the mountain was the only downside to the school, from a basketball perspective. The steep incline meant that students living in Burnaby weren't all that inclined to come back to school for games once they'd left campus in the evening.

Because the basketball team spent so much time in the gym, it made sense for us to live close to campus, rather than in the town of Burnaby itself. That decision was even easier because Coach Stewardson owned what was known as Basketball House—a huge, rambling place that he rented to his players for the grand total of $150 a month. There wasn't much living space at the top of the mountain where the campus was, but the house sat right at the bottom, as close as you could be.

My initiation to Basketball House came on my recruiting trip. I was hanging out in the house at about 10 p.m. on a Saturday night, and nothing much was happening, even though I'd been told it was a happening place. Back then, a lot of campuses had beer reps—guys whose job it was to supply beer for select parties and events. Tough job. Apparently one of their duties was to provide beer to Basketball House, and sure enough, the bathtubs that night were full of beer, but the house was empty, other than some of the guys on the team. I was still jet-lagged, so by 11 p.m., I was starting to fade.

"Guys, I might just go get some sleep," I said.

They looked at me as though I had just spoken a foreign language. "Don't worry," one of them said. "It's going to pick up." Sure enough, about half an hour later, the house started filling up, and by 2 a.m., it felt as though there were five hundred people inside. The music was pounding, and the floors were creaking from all the weight. I thought to myself, "So this is university."

As fun as the parties were, I was going to SFU for basketball, and Stan had done a great job recruiting me. After my introductory trip, I went back home for the summer, but there was never a week that went by that summer that I didn't get a poster or a letter or something to remind me of where I'd be that fall. He'd send me bumper stickers that I'd put on my school binders. That's not to say that I was the first skilled player to show up there—far from it. Stan had done a good job building the program, and a lot of his focus was on bringing in kids like me—players from Ontario who had finished grade thirteen and had that extra year of development behind them. It made the jump to NAIA (National Association of Intercollegiate Athletics) ball and playing US schools a lot easier.

Needless to say, I was pretty excited to start school that fall. After a hard summer of training with the Ontario provincial team, I packed up my stuff in August and moved across the country to pursue my dream. The only problem? Like a fool, I had arrived too early. I was so pumped up that I'd arrived more than a week before classes started. Every other student was enjoying his or her last week of summer freedom. Not me. I had moved across the country to set up in a massive empty house. It wasn't long before I was bored nearly to tears.

More than that, for the first time in my life I was lonely and homesick. I'd spent all of my life in Niagara Falls, surrounded by family and friends, a place where it felt as though everyone knew me and my family, where everywhere I went was familiar. In Niagara Falls, I never felt out of place. But in Burnaby, I didn't know where anything was or how to get there. This was my dream come true, right? I was exactly where I'd always thought I wanted to be, and I wished I could be anywhere else. I figured I'd made a huge mistake. So I trooped down to Stan's office—he was the only guy I knew in Burnaby at the time—and plopped myself down, about as bummed out as you can be. All I wanted to do was go home; I just couldn't quite figure out how I was going to tell him. As I debated how to break the news to him, he walked into the room with a man I hadn't met. Before I could open my mouth, Stan said, "Hey, Jay, I'd like you to meet Terry Fox."

You never know who is going to come into your life and when, or how he will affect it. The college years are about basketball, obviously, but so much more than that. You're growing up, and the people you meet are shaping you in ways you may not even appreciate. Sitting in Coach Stewardson's office that August day, a lonely college freshman far from home, how could I know that my life was changing at that very moment? Could I have imagined that I was starting a friendship with a Canadian icon to be, quite possibly the most widely revered individual of the past fifty years? Of course not. But even I was smart enough to figure out that this was not an ordinary teenager and it was time to keep my mouth shut.

The three of us chatted for a bit, and then Terry headed out. After Terry rolled his wheelchair away, I turned to Stan and said, "That's the guy who just—"

"Yeah," he said. "He just had the operation a little while ago."

"Man, I feel really bad. I didn't know what to say."

"You don't have to worry about that. Terry is going be your trainer this year. He was a part of the junior varsity team last year. He hurt his knee playing, but then they realized it wasn't an injury—it was cancer. He still wants to be part of the team, though, so you'll see him around a lot."

I was stunned. Seeing a nineteen-year-old kid in a wheelchair, his leg amputated at the knee—that sort of thing didn't happen to me every day. At that point, I'd heard of Terry, but he was a long way from becoming Terry Fox the national icon. He wasn't yet the guy who started the Marathon of Hope and became a national sensation in 1980. He was a curly haired kid with freckles from Port Coquitlam, British Columbia, who had played on the junior varsity team as a freshman at SFU the year before. We were the same age, but he was a year ahead of me because I had gone to grade thirteen. I had heard his story even before I met him. He was a heart-and-soul kid who had fallen down in practice and was complaining about a pain in his knee. The doctors had examined his knee, trying to figure out what the problem was. When they'd realized what was wrong, they had delivered the worst news an eighteen-year-old can hear: "Structurally your knee is fine; you didn't hurt your knee by falling down in practice, Terry, you fell down because your knee hurt, and your knee hurt because you have cancer."

"Well, what did you want?" Coach Stewardson asked. "Did you need something?"

At that point I wasn't going to complain about being homesick. Meeting Terry had given me a shot of reality.

"Not really. I just wanted to check to see if the gym was open," I said, making up an excuse on the spot. I went to the gym and started shooting, more appreciative than ever of the gifts I had been given.

27

The next day, I went back to the gym to shoot around, and Terry was there when I arrived. I immediately went over and we started getting to know each other—"How's everything going?," "Where are you from?," that kind of thing. It didn't take much to get Terry talking, and before long, he said, "Yeah, I'm going to run across."

I looked at Terry in his wheelchair. "Run across what?" I asked, trying to imagine how it would work.

"Canada," Terry replied. "I'm going to run across Canada."

What do you say to that? The last thing I wanted to be was rude to a guy I'd just met. But I had just flown from Toronto to Vancouver, and it had taken five hours. It was hard to imagine how anyone could run that far on two good legs. But that's what it's like when you meet a real dreamer in person: he's imagining his goal so powerfully that it's almost happened before it's started.

A few days later, the rest of the team showed up, and things quickly picked up. I discovered that living in Basketball House was the sort of thing you can go through only once. You're young, you're living with your buddies, and your only concerns are school, hoops, and the parties in between school and hoops. We had a party one night, and as I cleaned up beforehand, I picked up a plate of spaghetti that had been slid under the couch while we were watching *Sports Page*, the Vancouver sports highlights show that would come on at eleven o'clock every night. (That was way before on-demand sports highlights, so the 11 p.m. sportscast was essential viewing in the house. Sometimes you'd even get basketball highlights, imagine that.) I picked up the plate from under the couch, and I couldn't get the fork to separate from the plate. I kept yanking on the fork, and eventually the plate broke but the fork stayed stuck on. It wasn't the prettiest setup. But all we had to do was let the reps know we were having a party; they'd grab a key from us, and we'd go home after school to find all three bathtubs in the house full of free beer. We'd clean up afterward, return the cases of empties, and make enough money to go to the Keg for dinner. We felt like the richest guys in the world.

Tom Skerlak was my roommate in Basketball House. He had just come back from playing on the national team all summer, and as soon as he arrived, I started rattling off questions.

"Tom, what's it like?"

"It's great. We just got back from Bulgaria. Those guys are crazy!"

I tried to imagine Bulgaria on the map in my head, and I pictured the team taking to the floor surrounded by a loud Eastern European crowd. My foot started bouncing excitedly as I thought about the game.

"What are you doing right now? Want to go train?"

Tom laughed. "Sure, let's do it."

The facilities manager at the athletic centre, Kip Dougherty, was a grumpy, crusty former military guy. A lot of people were scared of him. But once he realized you were serious about your sport, he'd take you under his wing and he'd look out for you. Kip recognized that I wanted nothing more than to play basketball, so he gave me and Tom a key to the gym. We'd finish practice with the rest of the team, eat dinner, do some homework, and then get back to the gym late at night. We'd put on some music—Black Sabbath's "Iron Man" was one of our favourites, "Fly by Night" by Rush was another—and play crazy shooting games or one-on-one. Tom was from Welland, so we had our southern Ontario high school rivalry to draw from. We might drop in at the pub or something on the weekends, but then we'd go shoot. Tommy and I realized that if we wanted to reach our goals, we needed to get better and do the work.

Alex McKechnie was our fitness trainer. He was young in his career, and he always pushed us to our limit. The things he made us do weren't like anything else we'd experienced. We'd do wall sits, and Alex would come over and sit on our knees while we were squatting. Or he'd make us do commando crawls from one side of the gym to the other. One of his favourite exercises was a modified run up the hill. He'd take us to the bottom and pair us up. Then one partner would have to piggyback the other from the bottom of the mountain to the top. I'd carry my partner up as fast as I could until I couldn't do it anymore. Then we'd switch, and he would carry me. We would keep going like that, taking turns, until we got to the top, racing against your teammates and team building at the same time. Some of his workouts didn't even have anything to do with basketball. One day, he lined us up at the top of the hill.

"The exercise is simple," he told us. "Run to the bottom of the mountain, pick up a rock, and bring it back."

We all traded glances. That seemed pretty easy for a McKechnie workout. We waited for the other shoe to drop.

"Here's the catch: whoever comes back with the smallest rock goes back down and does it again." Without waiting for questions, McKechnie shouted, "Go!"

We sprinted to the bottom of the mountain and into the woods. As I searched for a rock, I looked around, trying to see who had a bigger rock. I had to pick a heavy rock, big enough that I wouldn't be last but small enough that I could still get up the mountain with it. By the time we got to the final incline, we were exhausted, trying to keep our balance on the rough terrain, thinking strategically and competing physically all at the same time. Later that night, as I lay stiff and sore on my bed, I realized how brilliant the exercise had been. It hadn't been about a physical workout; it had been about training our minds to make sure we were tougher and more resilient than anyone else.

We needed that mental training. We travelled for a lot of our games, and entering other schools' gyms—especially the ones in the United States—was like entering a lion's den. You had to trust in yourself and your team, and you had to be ready to compete all-out from the opening tip-off to the final whistle. I remember one of the first games I ever played was at Gonzaga University in Spokane, Washington. That was before it became a perennial NCAA power, but it was still a solid Division 1 program—all scholarship athletes, full gym, elite coaches. It was my first game as a freshman, and I wanted to make a statement. Early in the game, I stole the ball, sprinted down the court, and dunked it. When I dunked, I always took off from one foot—my high school high jump technique shining through—so in transition, I could dunk. I looked over, and my bench—the whole bench—was staring at me in shock. It wasn't like the cheering you see now, where everyone's holding each other back and waving towels. It was genuine shock, as though they had never seen anyone from Simon Fraser do that before, certainly not a rookie and certainly not against a D1 team on the road. We still lost the game, but the whole way home, guys passed me in the bus aisle, smiling and laughing to themselves as they muttered, "As if you just dunked at Gonzaga."

The next night, we were playing Montana State. I was standing in front of the sideline before the game, and the guy who was guarding me approached. Coach Stewardson walked up to the guy—who was a lot bigger and stronger than me—and looked him dead in the eye.

"This kid right here," Stan said, pointing at me, "he's going to fuck you up."

My opponent looked at Stan, unsure whether or not to believe him.

"He's fucking crazy, man," Stan continued. "He's going to fuck you up. Fucking crazy."

I didn't know what to do, so I just put my foot on top of the other guy's foot, and he backed away from me. The whole exchange was weird, but it reflected Stan's strategy—he always tried to convince us that we were tough, that we were better than we thought we could be, and he put us into positions where we had to back that up. It brought out the best in us, or at least in me. From that point on I pretended that I was tough, and, as Jack Donohue used to tell us, "fake it till you make it."

Terry didn't travel with us—he had to stay back for his treatments and training—but every time we got back from a trip, he was there, asking us how the games had gone. He taped our ankles, helped wash the uniforms, all the least glamourous jobs you can think of—pretty humbling for a guy who had been a player just a year before. He was a normal, everyday kid who happened to have had cancer and had half his leg cut off, who was going to run across the country to raise money for cancer research, and he didn't care all that much about what you or anyone else thought about it. That's one thing I will never forget. That whole history-making event was completely a product of one kid's imagination and ironclad will. When you witness something like that come together firsthand, it's hard not to believe that anything is achievable.

Terry was constantly positive, too. Early in the year, he organized an event to raise money. He rented the east gym on campus, and told us, "I'm having a big dance. A fundraiser to buy the van that I need to go with me. I'd love it if you guys came out."

When we arrived at the dance, the only other people there were from the women's basketball team. Terry had paid for everything—the gym rental, the food, the band—out of his own pocket, and we were nervous that nobody else had showed up.

"Terry, is anyone else coming?" I asked.

"They should be. And if they don't, it's okay—I'm going to have another one next week."

"What if no one shows up to that one, either? Aren't you losing money?"

But Terry wouldn't be discouraged. "We just got to have another one next week. They'll show up."

Sure enough, Terry threw another party the next week. A few more people showed up, but Terry didn't make any money. We thought that would be it, but just as he would do on his run, he never stopped. He threw a third dance the week after and another after that. By the fourth dance, the gymnasium was packed—everybody on campus wanted to go. There was no stopping Terry.

One Saturday morning, I was on the bus heading up to school. The hill up to campus is about a mile, straight up. I was feeling pretty good about myself—it might have been the weekend, but I was heading to the gym to do an extra workout, because, as I kept telling myself, I wanted to be an Olympian. I was congratulating myself on my hard work before I'd even left the house.

The bus engine had to grind to get up the mountain, and I could hear it straining and stressing through its gears as it crawled forward. I turned to look out the window on the way up, and whom did I see but curly haired, freckle-faced Terry Fox, rolling his wheelchair up the mountain. Talk about grinding. He was pushing and pulling for every foot of ground. "Holy shit," I thought to myself. "That's crazy."

A few minutes after I got to the weight room, Terry came in, dripping sweat.

"Did you just wheel up the mountain?" I asked.

"Yeah," he said. "I have to get my upper body strong. I only have strength in one leg now, so my upper body has to swing the prosthetic. It's hard coming up the mountain because I can't stop—if I stop, I roll back."

I'd known for a while that Terry was the real deal and that he was willing to put everything on the line to make his vision happen. If you can't draw some inspiration from that, there's something wrong with you. Having that living example of dedication, drive, and courage working and training alongside you—I can't quantify how much it contributed to me or my development, but it's never, ever left me. Not once. I don't have to dig too deep when things aren't going the way I would like them to. When I'm feeling a little down or overwhelmed, I just think of Terry wheeling himself up a mountain as training to run across Canada. It gets me back on task pretty quickly.

Of course, that was just the start of it. It was even more amazing when his run got going. Right before our eyes, this quiet, modest, determined kid turned into the best-known person in the country. One year, we were feeling bad for him because no one was at his school dance. The next, we were watching him on the news.

After Terry's cancer spread to his lungs and he stopped his run to come back home, he went to Simon Fraser to watch a few basketball games. The games were a break for him as he was going through his second round of treatment; they were something that felt normal, I suppose. After the first game he came to, I went up into the stands to catch up with him.

"The team's looking really good," he said. "Seems like you guys are heading in the right direction. Would you mind signing my program?"

"Terry, come on, man!" I said. "Why would you want my signature? You're the hero. I saw Darryl Sittler give you his jersey."

Terry laughed. "Oh, come on, you guys are going to do great things. I want to get your autograph now, before you get too famous."

Terry personified what the whole environment at SFU was about—being resilient, being tough, finding a way to be your best and doing even more than you might have thought you could. We were dreamers. It was an incredible four years. But what was most interesting wasn't the basketball. I'm incredibly proud of what SFU helped me accomplish and become, but that's not what I think about when I look back at that stage in my life. Individual records are nice accomplishments. But way more important are the lessons I learned there about being a teammate and what it takes to compete and be your best. I arrived there a homesick kid, ready to quit before I even started. But with one chance meeting, my life changed in an instant.

Simon Fraser made me a better basketball player, but I wanted bigger things. I wanted to play for my country, I wanted to be an Olympian, and basketball was only one part of the equation when it came to reaching those goals. How much everything else mattered I couldn't have known, but I was about to find out.

CHAPTER 3

JACK DONOHUE

After my first year at SFU, I got a call from one of my childhood coaches, a guy named Brian Mulligan. Brian had played in Niagara before becoming a coach in his own right. When I was a teenager, Brian had been like my big brother—he could deliver the right message in the right tone so that I would actively listen. He saw my excitement about the game, and he took me all over the place to play. For years, Brian was my ticket out of town. He even took me to my very first basketball camp. It was the summer before grade eleven, and I went to the Don Nelson–Satch Sanders basketball camp in Boston. Brian was going to work as a counsellor at the camp, and he took five of us from Niagara Falls along with him. It was the first time I had ever been on an airplane. More than that, it was the first time the world opened up for me a little bit. How was I supposed to know that people in Boston had their own unique accent, if not dialect? My first day at camp, I was nervous as hell, getting ready to play against a bunch of American kids. One of the coaches addressed the group in what I later realized was a thick Boston accent.

"Gods, I need all the gods over heah," he said.

At the clinics I'd been to, the coaches would divide the group into positions—forwards, centres, and, of course, guards. But I'd never heard anyone talk about gods before. I figured they were talking about people who were really good—the gods. *I think I'm pretty good*, I thought to myself. So I went to the right line—the one for guards, or whatever they called them in Boston—but not for the right reason. Hey, I hadn't been out of the Falls much.

When Brian called me that summer day, he was doing what he'd always done—looking out for me and helping me become the best player possible.

"Jay, I just heard that the Canadian national team is having an open tryout in a few weeks," he said.

"Seriously? Where?" I asked.

"Toronto. You need to be there. Do you think you can get back in time?"

"I wouldn't miss it!"

I headed back home and revved up my training in the weeks before the tryout. Making the national team as quickly as I possibly could was one of the reasons I had gone to SFU in the first place, so I wanted to make sure I was in the best shape possible. Everything seemed to be lining up perfectly, but then, one day before the tryouts, I sprained my ankle while training. It swelled up immediately. Perfect timing.

Under normal circumstances, I wouldn't have played for a few days at least, probably more like a couple of weeks. But I wasn't going to wait another year for my next chance to make the national team. So I called the trainer over.

"I need you to tape up my ankle."

"That's not going to help—you need to stay off it for a few days to let the swelling go down."

"I can't do that. Just tape it up as tight as you possibly can, because I'm not going to be able to redo it tomorrow."

I left the tape on the whole night and into the next day. The next morning, my ankle was throbbing, but I headed to Toronto for the tryout anyway. I didn't have a car, so Brian gave me a lift.

No surprise—I was horrible. I was trying to prove I was one of the best twelve or fifteen guys in the country, but I couldn't run or jump. Not a good formula. The tryout ended, and I knew I'd been terrible. There was not even a possibility I was going to be invited to training camp, let alone make the team.

I was silent as I made my way to the locker room. I sat down and finally hacked off the stinky, gooey tape, and my ankle ballooned. I knew I shouldn't have played, but all I wanted was a chance to make the national team. When I left, I was certain that I'd wasted my chance at realizing my dream.

What I didn't realize as I was sitting in the locker room, watching my ankle swell with each beat of my pulse, was that Don Mc-Crae had been observing me from across the room. Don was a very successful coach at the University of Waterloo and coached the Canadian women's team. After passing through the locker room, he headed upstairs, where the coaches were rehashing the tryout. Each coach was giving his input, but there was one person squarely in charge: Jack Donohue.

Jack had become the head coach of the Canadian national

team in 1972. He was American-born—a thick, burly New Yorker, complete with the accent and outsized personality to match. He'd started his coaching career at high schools in New York City. One of his earliest positions had been at Power Memorial Academy in Manhattan, where he had coached the future NBA star Kareem Abdul-Jabbar (Kareem was still known as Lew Alcindor then). At one point, the team had won seventeen consecutive games. He had then become head coach at College of the Holy Cross, a Division 1 school in Worcester, Massachusetts, before coming up to Canada to take over the national program.

I'd seen Jack coach throughout the 1976 Olympics, and I'd gotten to watch him coach in person during a game at Niagara University years before. Each game of his I watched, I was captivated by the way he patrolled up and down the sidelines like a general commanding his troops. To me, Jack was larger than life.

When my name came up in the coaches' room, Jack sounded off about how disappointed he'd been with my play.

"Yeah, that kid," Jack growled. "We had heard about him, but he wasn't that good."

I was supposed to be a hotshot Team Ontario kid playing with Simon Fraser, and I had looked like a total dud. But things happen in the strangest ways. Before Jack could move on, Don said, "I agree, he didn't play well. But I've seen him play better ball before, and I tell you what, you should see the size of his ankle. I was just down in the locker room, and he was taking this tape off and his ankle's the size of a grapefruit."

That seemed to get Jack's attention. Years later, Jack finally shared all of the details of the story with me. "What I remember is that you weren't good," he told me. "But I never saw you limp or make an excuse. You were hurt and it affected your game, but you didn't let it affect your attitude. That was impressive. The next time your name came up, we said, 'Yeah, let's have another look.'"

Needless to say, I didn't make the team that year, but my first national team experience lit a fire in me. Even though the tryout had been a disaster, I wanted to play for Canada more than ever. I went back to Simon Fraser and kept training my ass off over the course of the next season. The next summer, one year after my failed tryout, I was rewarded with an invitation to the national team training camp in Ottawa.

There is no comparison between what training camp was like then and what it is now. The attitudes toward training were fundamentally different. The old mentality was a little more militaristic— volume was king. For the most part, the guys were younger and none of them had professional commitments; unlike today, when so many of the players have to think about their NBA or professional careers before their national teams, at that time the Olympics were for amateur athletes only. A lot of us on the Canadian team were still in school, so the national team was the focal point of our whole basketball career. All of which is to say that when Jack stood in front of us in Ottawa and said, "You're going to have three practices a day for three days, and this is how we're going to pick the team," no one batted an eyelid.

That time, I was healthy and in great shape. I told myself that after the disaster of the previous year, this was going to be my time, and I would have nine chances over three days to prove myself.

But things never work out exactly as you plan, do they? The first practice, I couldn't make a shot. In fact, I didn't make a shot the whole morning. I was 0 for ninety minutes, or however long we practiced for. I was crushed. All that work. All that training. And when it counted, I couldn't put the ball through the basket.

We broke for lunch, but I was so upset that I couldn't even stomach food. *I blew it . . . again*, I thought. And things didn't get better. At the afternoon practice, I was even worse. I was supposed to be a shooter, the guy who could score in all kinds of ways, and I was laying bricks.

When the first day ended, it felt like a total write-off. I went back to my room and immediately called my parents.

"How is it going?" my mom asked.

"I didn't play very well."

"That's okay," she responded. "Tomorrow's another day." It was the sort of thing that moms are supposed to say, but I wasn't in the mood to hear it. I only had three days to prove myself, and on day one, all I'd done was show that I couldn't shoot. I was not in a very positive mood.

We said our good-byes, and I hung up the pay phone, looking around the bland university dormitory after one of the worst days of my basketball career. When I got back to my room, I lay down on my bed and tried to think about what I could have done better.

That's when a line from one of my childhood coaches drifted into my head: "How's the skin on your knees?" A competitor finds a way to contribute, regardless of whether or not his shots are falling. If contributing means losing some skin off your knees or elbows, so be it. I made a promise to myself to be better the next day.

On day two of the training camp, I got to the gym early and worked on my game. My shots were dropping, and I was feeling hot as shit. It seemed that the nerves were finally gone. But then the scrimmages started, and it was brick city again. Nothing was falling. I was on the verge of losing hope. *Maybe this national team thing isn't for me*, I thought.

But then I remembered what my coach had said. I looked up the floor, and there came a seven-footer. *Fuck this*, I thought, and *boom*, I stepped in front of him and drew the charge. The ball started to bounce out of bounds, so I jumped to my feet and dove on it. As I stood up, I noticed a little trickle of blood on my knee. *Yeah, that's what I want. Now I'm trying out.*

But I kept missing my shots. And the more I missed, the more crazed I became. I started diving for everything. The ball would bounce out of bounds, and the whistle would go, but I would run and dive on it when it was twelve feet out of bounds. Guys were asking me, "What are you doing?" But I didn't stop. I was grabbing guys on defence—if I wasn't going to score, you weren't going to score. I'd grab their shirt, chase them everywhere. I got four or five blocks. I couldn't score, but I went absolutely nuts. By the end of the second day, I was bruised and banged up, but I felt I had competed.

Then the third day came. I hadn't made a shot, which was what I was known for, but I went right back to doing all the other shit I'd done the day before. I never stopped. Part of it was because I was desperate, and part of it was because I was so mad at myself for shooting so badly.

Then finally, in the last practice—the ninth in three days—I came off a screen, caught a pass, let it fly, and it went in! Then I made another two or three shots right after it. Things were starting to flow a little bit. I ran back on defence, feeling great. But then I looked over at the sidelines, and the coaches were all huddled up. They hadn't even been watching the last scrimmages. They had already decided who they were going to take, so what happened in the final game was irrelevant—they had seen what they needed to see.

I was crushed. I felt I had wasted my second straight national team tryout. After practice ended, I went back to my room and started packing my bag. There were fifty guys there, and the coaches were going to pick twelve. There was no way that one of those spots would go to a shooter who couldn't shoot.

As I left my room, I looked down the hall of the dorm and saw a group of guys gathered around the list of twelve guys who had made the team, posted on a door. Some of the guys from Simon Fraser were there, and as I got closer, I could hear some muttering "This is bullshit" and "Fuck, *he* made the team? I can't believe it."

Who are they talking about? I wondered. I finally got close enough to see the list, and my name was on it. It was right there in black and white. The guy who couldn't hit a shot. I was one of the twelve guys they were taking on the national team. I tried to be cool. I didn't want to embarrass anyone who wasn't on the list. I walked calmly back to my room, unpacked my stuff, then grabbed the phone and started calling everybody I knew. "I made Canada's national team!" I yelled over and over. Then I started phoning people I didn't know. I was just dialing random numbers, saying "I made Canada's national team," and hanging up. I was so happy.

The euphoria lasted barely twenty-four hours. The next day was a shot of reality, thanks to Jack, who wasn't big on sugarcoating. We were at our first team meeting—my first team meeting as a member of the Canadian national team—and I was still on cloud nine. But then Jack started speaking.

"Let me tell you how we picked this team," he said. "We identified the top five guys, the five guys we think are going to start. We think those are the five best players. And the next five are going to be the guys who are going to be the backups if anybody gets hurt or gets into foul trouble. Those next five are very important. Number eleven and number twelve aren't going to play."

In just a few seconds, I'd gone from elated to embarrassed. Sure, I was on the team, but I'd just been told that I wasn't going to play. And Jack wasn't done. He turned to his assistant coach, Steve Konchalski, a fellow New Yorker. Steve knew his lines.

"Steve, where do we have number eleven and number twelve ranked among the fifty players at training camp?" Jack asked.

"I'm not sure," Steve said.

"No, we ranked them all. Where do we have them ranked?"

"They were somewhere between thirty-five and forty-five on our list." Now there was no doubt about where I stood.

"That's right. But what we did is, we picked the two players that worked harder than anybody else. Because if they work that hard every single day, they're going to make the bench players better, and they're going to make the starters better. I can't get twelve guys in a game. So I picked the two guys that work harder than anybody else."

That hurt to hear. But as much as it stung, I did see some wisdom in Jack's words. I might not have liked it, but at least I knew what my role was. So every practice, I did exactly what Jack had said: I worked my ass off. I knew I wasn't going to play in the games, so the practices became my games. It was an invaluable time. I travelled around the world. I hung out with an amazing group of guys and tried to enjoy everything about it.

Before one of our first games, Jack called me over and said, "You sit beside me, and you tell me what's working and what's not working. You write down the name of the play and a check mark if we

45

score or an X if we don't." Basically, my job was going to be to keep stats during games. That wasn't all I did, though. During warm-ups, the starters would shoot around, and I was the rebounder. I almost never even put up a shot, but I'd ask the starters, "Do you want me to put a hand in your face or not?" I'd rebound their shot, snap a pass to the next guy, and then run out and put a hand in their face, playing shadow defence. At the end of the shootaround, when everyone else was sitting down and taking their shoes off, it was time for me to run—sprints, back and forth, sideline to sideline, while everyone else was done and relaxing. It wasn't the most glamourous role, but I made the most of it. Jack was always changing the eleventh guy—one week, a guy from the bench would be bumped down, and then the next week, someone else would be in the doghouse. But the twelfth man? That was always my spot.

I eventually got enough nerve to talk to Jack about my chances. "Any chance that I can move up?" I asked.

"No. You're doing a hell of a job, let me tell you. You're doing a great job with the stats, and you're real positive. I give those guys shit when they come off the floor. You're always giving them a towel and a glass of water. They really like you. Some of those other guys that we've got rid of, they're at the end of the bench, and they're bringing somebody else down. They're saying 'I should be playing. I'm better than this guy.' You've never said anything negative like that. You're just positive. We really like what you're doing."

It was nice to hear, but I still wanted to play. We'd be up 30 against Argentina or down 30 against Brazil, and Jack would yell "Triano!" I would rip off my sweats and run down, thinking he was calling me to check in to the game. Instead, Jack would say, "No, no, no, no, how are we doing in high post?"

"We're three for four."

"Okay, sit back down." Then he'd shout to the guys on the floor, "Stay with high post!" I'd go back to my seat and keep charting plays.

For two years, I kept fulfilling my responsibilities as the twelfth man. It certainly wasn't how I had pictured my national team career unfolding, but there were some great lessons there. I'd made the team as a hard worker, even though I couldn't make a shot. And I stayed on the team because I was a good guy. Those are qualities anybody can have, in whatever walk of life. Work hard, regardless of the result? Anyone can do that. Be a good guy, even if you may not be getting the results you think you should be? That's under your control, too.

Don't get me wrong, I was dying to play. When I'd dreamt of playing in the Olympics, I was hitting the game winner to earn a medal, not keeping stats at the end of the bench. The one expression you hear over and over again in the NBA is "Stay ready." As a coach, you are constantly communicating some version of that message to guys who are outside the rotation. It is hard to stay at your peak, mentally and physically, when you are almost never playing and never know when you're going to play. But if you're a reserve player, that is quite literally your job. And guys who can do that make their way ahead. In my years in the NBA, I've seen it so many times: guys who have been really diligent about their preparation and who shine when they get a chance to play due to injury or suspension or whatever. The flip side is true, too: guys who let their preparation and attitude slip because they allow themselves to get discouraged about their role, and then, when their moment comes, aren't ready, or never get their moment because the coaching staff won't trust them or reward their lack of effort. It's no exaggeration to say that careers can be made or broken by how guys handle themselves when they're not playing regularly. It happens all the time.

My break came in the summer of 1980 in San Juan, Puerto Rico. It was the qualifying tournament for the 1980 Olympic Games in Moscow. Jack had been running his program in Canada for nearly a decade at that point, so we had an excellent team—the core of it had finished sixth at the World Championships in 1978—made up of experienced veterans and young talent. We had some good size, too, and, of course, we had me, holding a clipboard but trying to stay ready.

When Varouj Gurunlian took a charge in a game against Cuba, he took a knee to his ribs and broke them. Our starting two-guard was now out for the tournament. That wasn't a problem, though, because his backup, Donald "Doc" Ryan, was a really good player. Ryan was very physical and smart—he went on to become a successful CIS (Canadian Interuniversity Sport) coach—so we were going to be okay. I was now one step up on the depth chart, mind you, but not necessarily closer to playing. Chances were that Jack was going to play Doc straight for forty minutes.

There are few places hotter than a basketball court in Puerto Rico, even in April. The sweat running off the guys would have filled buckets. Unfortunately, after Varouj Gurunlian went down, they didn't wipe up all of the sweat on the floor. On his first play after checking in, Doc, without even the benefit of getting a proper warm-up, tried to change direction, slipped on the wet spot, and blew out his knee. Within one minute of game time, we'd lost both of our two-guards for the remainder of the tournament, if not the summer.

After Doc went down, I heard Jack yell, "Triano!"

I ran down the bench with my clipboard and told him, "Stay with the high post, it's working."

"No, you're going in," Jack replied.

I stood there, shaking. I had barely played a minute of international basketball—we'd had so few games to prepare that every minute was precious, so there was no such thing as "garbage time" where Jack would just roll out his subs. Everything was about the greater mission. The last time I'd actually been in a game was in a pretournament game before the World Championships two years earlier, when we had been playing against the Filipino national team on its home court. I'd gotten into the game very late, and a shot had gone up. I'd crashed the boards, all excited. But I was late getting to the rebound, and my timing was all off. The ball hit the rim, and as I jumped, for some reason, I decided to try to shoot it without coming back to the floor—a put-back, I guess. I got the ball, but I second-guessed myself and landed. I jumped back up again, but I still had the arm part of the shot in my mind, so when I added my legs, I shot the ball way too hard. It peaked way above the net, hit the top of the backboard, and landed out of bounds on the other side. All that from about eight feet away. I'm not sure how you can miss a shot worse than I missed my first—and to that point, only— shot as a national team player.

That game against the Philippines had been a warm-up, but now we were in the middle of a game that really mattered.

"Now? You ask me now?" I said to Jack. I was terrified.

"Just play the same way you do in practice every single day."

With that I went in. As I stepped onto the floor, I felt a calm settle over me. The fear—of losing, of not pulling my weight—was there. But I knew what I had to do. I ended up leading the team in scoring that game, and we beat Cuba by 3. Not only that, but we went 5–1 in the tournament, finished second, and qualified for the Olympics.

How does such a thing happen? Is it fate? Is it hard work? Is it luck? There is no doubt that I had done my best to "stay ready." The fact that I had to draw the plays every game, check them, and track our success rate meant that I knew every play. And the extra running? I was in shape. Because we'd had no backup for the rest of the tournament, I had played forty minutes a game. I had done my work, even though I'd never expected to play, and it had paid off. I was optimistic that I might be able to keep earning my playing time during the actual tournament.

But then, just two days after we qualified for the Olympics, we heard that, due to the Soviet Union's invasion of Afghanistan, Canada wouldn't be going to the Olympics. Prime Minister Pierre Trudeau decided to support the US-led boycott of the Games, and just like that, forty-eight hours after achieving an incredible high, we were set back for reasons we had no control over. It was crushing—to this day, I haven't fully gotten over it. Brazil, which we had just beat in San Juan, ended up going in our place and won a bronze medal.

It was a lot to process at the time. I had just played some of the best basketball of my life, and after the news came in, I sat with Jack in our individual meetings.

"This is so disappointing. Just after I finally got a chance to play," I said. I was feeling pretty proud of myself. It wasn't like "I showed you," but it was satisfying to come through in that kind of situation and justify my place on the team beyond being a hard worker and a good guy who could handle a clipboard.

But instead of offering sympathy or praise, Jack just said, "Don't get fat."

"What do you mean?" I asked.

"I don't expect you to actually get fat, but it's a terminology that we have. Don't forget how you got to where you are now. Be the same person, be the same player, and you'll be fine."

I was about to ask Jack what he meant, but he cut me off. "You're going to be with me a long time. But I've got to talk to some guys who are getting older and who might not get another chance to go to the Olympics. Martin Riley, Tom Bishop, Ross Quackenbush. These guys aren't going to get another opportunity to play. You're going to get a chance to play again."

It was powerful. When you're young, sometimes you're so caught up in proving yourself that you don't think about other people's situations. Jack's perspective struck a chord. I had had a great individual moment, but the moment wasn't about me.

Despite my disappointment at not going to the Olympics, that taste of what it was like to play for my country, the uncertainty of international basketball, the sense of mission I had with my teammates—it was intoxicating. And as devastating as it was to have to boycott the Games in Moscow, it was fuel to make sure we qualified again. Playing for Canada was everything for me. I loved the feeling of being so far away from home, representing my country with a band of brothers. It was an adventure and gave basketball a sense of purpose for me. You're not playing for yourself—it's bigger than that. Once I got a taste of that experience, I discovered it was better than I'd expected in all those years I'd spent dreaming about it, and it became all I wanted. Even as I was progressing through Simon Fraser, as important as that experience was for me, and as close as I was to the guys on the team and to Terry, the national team was always in the back of my mind.

Although my sights were set squarely on Canada, the wider basketball world soon came knocking. After my senior year at SFU, I went back to Ottawa to train with the national team for another season. It was June 1981, and the NBA draft was approaching, but, although I was finishing university, I had given little thought to a pro career. I was still focused on the Canadian national team.

No one called me before the draft or brought me in for a workout or an interview. These days, it's not all that unusual for a guy who played college basketball in Canada to at least get an invitation to an NBA summer league roster. There are very few secrets anymore. But the basketball landscape was so much different then. The NBA had ten rounds in which to draft players, compared with two today (although there were only twenty-two teams doing the drafting, compared with thirty), and the means of identifying players who weren't in the traditional pipeline weren't as advanced as they are now. Among social media, YouTube, the breadth of international basketball right down to the under-16 age group, and the emphasis on finding players off the beaten path, it's hard to imagine someone with an NBA skill set not being identified at some point. There are just too many eyes on the game and too many ways to share information for a good player not to be on someone's radar.

In my draft year, though, scouting was a lot more word of mouth. Someone might mention a name to a friend, there would be a few phone calls, that kind of thing. For the Canadian scene, a lot of that talk went through Jack, who was very well connected to the NBA from his days in New York City.

Sure enough, after one of our three-practices-a-day sessions,

Jack pulled me aside and said, "The draft is today. I've had a couple of teams call and ask about you. So you might get drafted."

Cool, I thought. But that was the extent of the hype, and I remained doubtful. The NBA had never really been a goal of mine, so I wasn't too caught up in what might happen at the draft.

I didn't have a direct link to the draft or a way of following it, so I didn't know the results until twenty-four hours later, when the news finally made its way up to us. Jack came up to me at practice the next day, saying, "I got a phone call. You got drafted by the Lakers in the eighth round."

"That's great!" I said.

"No, you know what's really great about it is that the Lakers weren't even one of the five teams that called me and that I recommended you to. That means that there were more teams out there that knew you. That's what's really good." It turned out there was a Lakers area scout who watched college basketball in the Pacific Northwest and who'd come across me when I was at Simon Fraser.

I was the 179th player taken overall, so I can't say I felt as though an NBA career was around the corner. But a chance to play on the team's summer league team was exciting. The summer league head coach was a Lakers assistant coach by the name of Pat Riley. He was a very young coach at the time—he didn't become *the* Pat Riley until he took over from Paul Westhead early in the 1981–82 season. Even as a young guy, though, Pat was a very good coach. Great presence. Very demanding, even in that summer league setting. Just a strict, hard-nosed guy. He wanted things done his way, which you could respect.

The Lakers were just a season removed from winning the NBA championship in 1980 and were obviously one of the best teams in basketball. I had no reason to expect that I would make the team—they weren't about to start handing out roster spots to any eighth-round picks. Still, it was one of those "pinch me"–type memories.

Every day, I and the other prospective rookies and free agents— it wasn't as though Magic and Kareem were scrimmaging with us—trained at the Forum in Inglewood, California, near LA. We were staying at a hotel right across the street, so our days were confined to that little bubble as we went back and forth between hotel and arena.

Still, there were plenty of ways to entertain ourselves. Each day, one of the team officials would come by and give us an envelope with our per diem cash in it. One day, Kevin McKenna—who ended up coaching at Creighton University in the NCAA—said, "I'm going to go to the racetrack. Who wants to join?" I wasn't a big pony guy, but it sounded like fun, and we all needed the diversion.

Another day, we were sitting around after a meal, and Kevin said, "What are you doing tonight? There's a concert at the Forum, and we can get in free."

It wasn't just any concert. As part of his contract with the Lakers, Kareem Abdul-Jabbar got the Forum one night a year for a free concert. The salary cap hadn't been invented yet, so it was a perk the team had offered to him. Tom Petty and the Heartbreakers were playing that night, so off we went.

That was just the start, though. A couple of days later, I was having some problems with tendonitis in my knee. It wasn't major, but I headed over to see the trainer, a guy named Sparky, at the Forum before practice. As I walked into the Lakers' training room, I saw a guy on the table next to me having his ankle worked on. He was laid out with towels all over his head, so I couldn't tell who it was or if he was even awake. I chatted quietly with Sparky, and finally there was some movement on the other table. The guy pulled the towel off his head, revealing long blond hair. He sure didn't look as though he was there to try out for the Lakers.

"What the fuck's up, man?" he asked in a raspy voice.

"How you doing?" I asked.

"Not good! Look at this fucking thing," he said, pointing at his ankle. "I did a back flip off the speaker last night in San Francisco and wrecked my ankle." His ankle did look bad—I definitely wouldn't have played basketball on that thing. "I gotta get on the fucking stage tomorrow, and this fucking thing's killing me."

"The stage?" I asked. "What do you do?"

"I'm a musician. Name's David, nice to meet you," he said, extending his hand.

"I'm Jay," I said, now realizing that I was shaking hands with David Lee Roth, the lead singer of Van Halen.

We talked for a while as the trainers worked on our legs. Roth seemed to think I was a player with the Lakers, as opposed to an eighth-round pick from Niagara Falls putting in his time in summer league. I was in Lakers gear, getting treatment from the Lakers' trainer, so I wasn't about to correct him.

Roth had a lot of respect for the athletes. At one point, he said, "What I do, what you do, it's the same fucking thing. We're, like, both entertainers. You gotta do what you gotta do. You're trying to get healthy, I'm trying to get healthy."

After my treatment, I went back to the hotel. I was sitting at the pool when Roth and the band members walked onto the patio. All of a sudden, a waiter appeared beside me holding a Corona.

"It's on me, man!" Roth said as he walked over. "By the way, do you want to go to the show tonight? I've got a couple backstage passes."

I wasn't going to say no. A few hours later, my roommate and I were backstage, watching Van Halen do their thing. *So this is the NBA life*, I thought.

After the show, Roth invited us to the after-party back at the hotel. My roommate and I got on the elevator, and when the doors opened to the band's floor, it looked, smelled, and sounded exactly like you might expect Van Halen's after-party to look, smell, and sound after a show in LA. My buddy and I looked at each other. I'm sure there was a good time to be had, but I just said, "I think we better push 'down,'" and we went back to our room.

As fun as the Lakers' summer team was, I never felt as though I was going to make the main team in the fall. More than that, though, I never seemed to be able to get my mind off of what might be happening with the national team back in Ottawa. A few weeks into the summer league, I had a meeting with Pat.

"Pat, thank you for everything you've done for me and for the chance to come and play here," I said. "But I need to head back to Ottawa. The national team is headed to Romania soon to play, and I want to be there with them."

Pat was a little surprised. It was not something he was used to hearing every day, I guess. "I was going to give you a little more time," he said.

"I appreciate that, but let's be honest, I'm not making the Lakers this year."

"It's your decision," Pat said.

It sounds kind of funny now—passing up on hanging out in LA

and preparing with the Lakers so I could go to Romania—but the national team was where my heart was. So I went back to Carleton and started training again with Canada.

My time in LA had been productive, though. Those three weeks of playing in a professional environment—even though it was summer league and not the regular NBA roster—had made a big difference in my game. On my first day back, Karl Tilleman, the sharpshooting University of Calgary star, said to me, "I can't believe how after three weeks you could get that much better." I had been playing against NBA-calibre guys every day, learning from them and building my confidence. I realized that I could match up well against guys who had come out of big-time programs and even against guys who already had pro experience. I had come a long way in a short period of time.

As a kid, I'd needed a ride to my first national team tryout from Brian Mulligan, and I'd gotten a chance only because I had busted my ass and hadn't complained. But when I came back to the national team after my three weeks in LA, I was a different player. A different person. I couldn't be stopped. I felt I could do whatever I wanted to.

CHAPTER 4

MIRACLE ON HARDWOOD

Ever since Jack had taken over the national team in 1972, his goal had been to build a team that could win gold medals on the international stage—something Canada had never done. We'd missed out on the podium at the 1976 Olympics, but we weren't going to let that stop us. Jack wasn't going to let that stop us.

Things began coming together in 1981. I was a regular fixture on the national team by then, and that year, I was named captain. It was an indescribable honour—I'd always wanted to serve as a leader on the team, and I would have done anything for my teammates. Day to day, being named captain didn't mean much. There was no public announcement or "C" emblazoned on my jersey. But I felt a new fire burning inside me.

We were a young team—we'd been together for only twenty-three days—but we had enough holdover from the team that had qualified for the Olympics in 1980 to feel some cohesion as we set out for the World University Games that summer. The games were being held in Bucharest, Romania, behind the Iron Curtain—a less-than-ideal vacation spot at the time—but that was par for the course with the national team back then. Though every international trip was different, the conditions we played under usually left something to be desired, and Bucharest didn't deviate from that. The cafeteria was fairly bare, and the cheese and cold cuts that were sitting out had flies hovering over them. There was no such thing as energy bars, so we'd learned to take lots of peanut butter along and hope the bread was somewhat edible. We'd all lose weight. The living quarters weren't any better. We bunked up in student dormitories, but the mattresses were thin and our legs hung over the ends of the beds. I bunked with Bill Wennington, who would go on to have a storied NBA career, winning three championships with the Chicago Bulls and setting screens for some guy named Michael Jordan. Somehow Bill and I stumbled across a fridge in the dorms, and we decided to "borrow" it for our room so we could keep some drinks cold. It felt like a luxury.

A lot of times what was going on off the court was just as interesting as the competition. Before we headed to Romania, our team doctor, Andrew Pipe, tried to educate us about what day-to-day life was like in Communist countries. Of all the things he told us, the point that stood out most was that there was a black market for cigarettes. We saw the opportunity to make a little cash and packed as many cartons of cigarettes into our luggage as we could. We were feeling pretty entrepreneurial as we sold packs of cigarettes through the fence of the athletes' village for $10 until Stewart Granger, our point guard, did us one better. Most of us were from small towns, where we were lucky to have had a coach who had turned us on to basketball before the sport became so popular. But Stewie, who had been born in Montreal, had grown up in Brooklyn, and he was tough and brash and street smart. He thought that if people were willing to spend $10 on a pack of twenty cigarettes, they might be willing to spend $2 on a single cigarette. Next thing we knew, he was making $40 for one pack. Leave it to the New York kid on the team to figure that out.

In two years, Stew would be the twenty-fourth draft pick and play for the Cleveland Cavaliers, but in 1981, he was fresh from Philadelphia's Villanova University and had zero respect for our American competitors. For the rest of us, it was hard not to be at least a little bit intimidated by the Americans. The United States was the heart of basketball culture—its college games were what we saw on Canadian television, and unlike us, its college players played in front of thousands of fans each night, were seen as heroes on their campuses, and were coached by big names in basketball. They were the ones on the cover of *Sports Illustrated*. But Stewie didn't care. He'd beaten most of them during his college career.

I'd be walking through the athletes' village with Stew, and he'd see John Pinone, his teammate at Villanova, playing for Team USA. "Johnny P, we're going to kick your ass!" he'd yell. He knew we were good, and he wasn't scared.

The team needed that kind of confidence. Jack continually tried to work on dismantling the inferiority complex we had when it came to basketball and the Americans. When we came out flat against the Americans at the Pan Am Games in 1979, he told us that he was going to send us all home on the spot. Jack had a clear message for us: produce on the floor, or I'll replace you.

In the six years that Jack had been head coach of the national team, the program had come a long way, but there was still one more hurdle we needed to get over—beating the Americans—and it was as much mental as anything else. Jack was American, but he believed in us. We just needed to believe in ourselves, which was no easy task, especially in Bucharest, where the odds felt stacked against us. In any sport—wrestling, volleyball, you name it—the US and Canadian competitors were on the same side of the draw, which meant the Romanians and other Soviet bloc teams had a better chance of advancing to the medal rounds. In basketball, we were in a pool—the Toilet Bowl, as we called it—with the United States, Mexico, and the Soviet Union, but only two teams could advance to the Rose Bowl, i.e., the medal round. Now was the time to show Jack and ourselves what we could do.

We got on a roll during our first few games. Undefeated in the preliminaries, we were feeling quietly confident—or, in the case of Stew, loudly confident—as we faced off against the United States in our first game of the qualification round. The game itself was tense and competitive, as though a bar fight were about to break out at any moment. Maybe it's a hockey mentality or something, but we always played close to the edge and a few guys would gladly have stepped over.

For the first half, we controlled the game, leading most of the way. If Canada had any identity in world basketball in those years, it might have been that: turn up the temperature at your own risk; we might even turn it up for you. As we moved into the final quarter, we were up by 8 points, and we could feel the Americans getting frustrated.

Our centre, a big kid from Montreal named Rick Hunger, got

into it with his counterpart, Fred Roberts, who played at Brigham Young. I'm not sure what Fred did, but it was enough to start a fight in front of the US bench. Chaos erupted as the floor filled with players from both teams and even some fans. It took about ten minutes before the game could start again, and when it did, we were rattled. The United States went on a run and tied the game with six minutes remaining. But we were able to calm ourselves. I hit a jumper, and Stew stayed cool running the point. I hit another jumper with just over a minute to play, and Stew sealed it with one of his own.

We'd done it! We'd won! We'd beaten the Americans on a diet of peanut butter and rock-hard bread. Our confidence swelled. Everything Jack had been pushing us toward seemed possible.

On our way back to the village, Stewie didn't hold back. When he saw the Americans, he called, "We kicked your ass, man!"

It felt great.

But the feeling didn't last long. In international basketball, points matter as much as wins and losses. Jack knew that better than anyone. "Every play, every possession counts," he would say. "If we're winning by ten, we have to win by twelve. If we're down by twenty, we have to cut the lead, even by a few points."

But it was hard to take that in when we were coming off of a major victory. Still, while the rest of us were basking in the glow of a win, Jack was focused on the bigger picture. "Points carry over in the event of a tiebreaker," he reminded us.

We beat the United States by four points, but in our next game, we lost to the Soviet Union by the same number. The Americans and the Soviets played each other next in a game that went to overtime, and the Americans won by, again, four points.

At the end of the round, we were even with the United States and the USSR, each of us holding a 2–1 record. Our total points scored were divided by the total points scored against us, and when the math was done, we finished third by 0.05 point—the Soviet Union had beaten Mexico by just slightly more than we had. Jack was right. Every free throw, turnover, basket, stop, or missed assignment against the other countries mattered. One point was the difference between us playing for a medal and playing for fifth.

The Americans let us have it in the village. "You're playing for fifth place, Stewie. Then you're going home."

Stew got pretty heated. "If this was the NCAA, you'd be home already, we beat your ass."

He was right, but this wasn't the NCAA. It was international basketball. The rules might have been strange, they might have been different, but they were the rules of the game. You have to respect them, accept them, and play to them, or all the complaining in the world is just pissing in the wind. In any given game, you never know what the turning point might be. For the rest of our years together as a team, whenever someone would make a lazy play in a practice or forget an assignment, Jack would let him know how thin the line was.

"Remember Romania," he'd say. "That could be the difference between playing the Rose Bowl or the Toilet Bowl."

Even though we were disappointed, we went home with a win over the United States, something no Canadian team had ever done before. Our win didn't get a lot of attention—there was no press conference at the airport, no media circuit reliving the game. But we didn't care. It was time to move on and build on what we'd accomplished, and our eyes were on the 1982 World Championships in Bucaramanga, Colombia. For the first time, we believed we could win a spot on the podium.

We had an incredibly talented team that included Stew, Bill, and Leo Rautins, all strong players who went on to be first-round picks in the NBA draft. We started our season playing in Taiwan in the R. William Jones Cup, but things went downhill fast. Jack got very sick, and our manager, Ed Brown, had to step in to coach. He was a wonderful guy, but he wasn't the head coach and he was battling cancer—tragically, he would pass away shortly after the tournament. We were maturing together as a team but still lacked self-discipline—we were a bunch of young guys who wouldn't be herded. There's always the option to get into trouble overseas, and it takes only one or two guys who are more focused on partying in a distant land than competing on the court to tip the balance on a team and dilute the focus the team needs to excel. Needless to say, the trip to Taiwan got us off on the wrong foot.

Still, we had reason to be confident. At the World's Fair in Knoxville, Tennessee, we beat the United States and Yugoslavia—both gold medal favourites. What the average fan may not know is that trying to upset Yugoslavia was considered as difficult a feat as taking down the United States. Perhaps that success worked against us. We were no longer under the radar, and by the time we made it to Colombia for the World Championships, we were treated as a threat, and although Jack was back, as a team we weren't properly focused on the task at hand.

It showed on the court, where our play was chaotic. We did well enough in the first round against Uruguay, but we needed an amazing 31-point, ten-assist game to win against Czechoslovakia to advance to the second round. We relied on Stew to call plays and direct us on the court, and he put everything out on the floor to bring us the win. Next up, Yugoslavia.

Tensions were high and the score was close, but the crowd was on our side. Whenever we scored a basket, they would erupt in cheers. We were trailing by 4 late in the first half of the game when I got loose on a clear fast break. I jumped for a layup, but my legs were taken out from me, which is one of the most dangerous plays in basketball. When a player leaves the ground, he's vulnerable, and if he's undercut by another player, he can't control how he lands. Anything can happen, from a broken wrist to a broken neck. I ended up smashing into the end wall, and when I turned around, I saw Stew come down on the guy who had undercut me and start fighting.

After the refs broke up the fight, they ejected Stew from the game for elbowing the Yugoslavian player. It was a terrible call—the Yugoslavians had started the whole mess, and our most important player was gone. The crowd knew it, too, and began booing and littering the floor with coins and whatever else they could grab to show their displeasure with the officials. It was mayhem. The game was stopped for fifteen minutes, and the Yugoslavians left the floor until the riot police showed up. Eventually the game started up again, and we lost a tough-fought battle to one of the best teams in the world.

Jack was convinced that Stew had been targeted by the officials, who had tossed him out the first chance they got. I guess all those years playing internationally kind of conditioned us to expect the worst outcome possible. We'll never know for sure, but Stew was suspended for the following game against the Soviet Union, which we lost. Australia then upset us in the semifinal round, which meant we were in the classification round again, eventually finishing sixth. It was a frustrating way to end the summer, to say the least.

Jack took our exit from the tournament hard. He blamed himself for giving us too much leash, but his coaching philosophy had always been grounded in trusting us and treating us like professionals, which meant he didn't enforce curfews and other off-court rules. In Jack's mind, if we needed those rules, we probably didn't have the discipline we needed to succeed. All of us, including Jack, learned important lessons from that experience that changed how we operated and set us up well for the future.

We realized that talent wasn't everything. There's no question that Jack took the best twelve players from our 1982 camp. But we weren't the best team, because we didn't have twelve guys who completely bought into what was best for the group, who were singularly focused on basketball, and who would do whatever it took to compete on the international stage. We just didn't have the right fit. After our defeat at Worlds, Jack chose the guys who he thought would play best together as a unit, rather than simply the best players available, and he continued to do so for the rest of the years I played for him. Talent was only one part of the equation.

Another part was practice. Jack was old school. His values were to put the team first, share the ball, and do the work. If practicing once a day was good, then two-a-days were better. We had grueling training camps where we practiced morning, noon, and night.

Jack was ahead of his time in some ways. He understood the emotional and mental challenges of high performance, and he cared about how we handled the stress, so he brought in Cal Botterill, a sports psychologist who had worked with Canada's national hockey team, to help us tap into what made us perform our best and to limit our distractions and manage our emotions. He had a very reassuring energy, and he showed us how to use pressure as an opportunity to succeed.

When the team got back together in the summer of 1983, we had a very clear objective: the World University Games in Alberta. We knew that tournament wasn't the Olympics or even the World Championships, but it felt just as special to us because it was a chance to win a medal in our home country.

We spent the summer in the dormitories at the University of Alberta. Literally. Because outside in the prairie heat were swarms of bloodthirsty mosquitoes so big we wondered if they were some kind of prehistoric birds come to life from a fossil in the oil sands. The dorms were our refuge, and basketball was our mission. In the gym and on the floor, we were on point, at the ready for anything that might come our way at the World University Games. It didn't matter that we were trapped inside; we weren't bored. I was twenty-five years old with a full head of hair, spending the summer with my best friends making plans to kick ass and listening to music on Bill's portable stereo.

Bill, who is seven feet tall and rocked a flowing mullet, carried his boom box everywhere. One time we were in New York City for a game, and Bill—a pretty big star at St. John's University in Queens at the time—walked down the street with his stereo on his shoulder, blasting the radio at full volume. Today in the NBA, it's fifteen guys, fifteen phones. Everyone is in his own little world. That was not an option in 1983 or any of the other years I played. We were in one another's lives every minute of every day.

Our theme song was "Sail On" by the Commodores. We'd listen

to it nonstop, walking to practice or back from a shootaround. It was our soundtrack. The song is about a small-town kid picking himself up after disappointment and staying confident that the best is yet to come. Fit us to a T.

Why would a bunch of twenty-something basketball players choose a piano ballad about a bad breakup as an anthem? There's really no good answer other than that things like that just happen when you're on a team. We spent so much time together that we weren't trying to be cool anymore. We knew one another too well for that. When I looked around the locker room, I knew everyone like a brother. Jack had done that. The national team was more a family than a team, and each member was ready to accept whatever role Jack needed him to. We felt as though we were ten feet tall and bulletproof. We were going to sail on.

When the World University Games began in earnest, we were prepared. We'd had our usual three-week training camp in Ottawa and then a five-game exhibition tour against several different countries, with games in Ottawa, Toronto, Vancouver, Victoria, and finally Lethbridge in Alberta, where we played the United States. It had a really good team that year, with two future Hall of Famers and a slew of other soon-to-be NBA stars, including Charles Barkley (aka Sir Charles), Karl Malone (aka King Karl), Ed Pinckney, Kevin Willis, Jay Humphries, and Johnny Dawkins. We ended up losing in overtime, but that just confirmed for us that we could hold our own with the top teams. Sir Charles even said that he wasn't looking past us: "If we don't play as well as we can, the gold will stay in Canada."

We started the tournament in a pool with Yugoslavia, Angola, Jordan, China, and Israel. We didn't want to play the United States until the final round, so our plan was to win our pool and play whatever team the United States defeated. The preliminary round went as well as could be expected. We won easily against Angola, Jordan, and China, but we lost to Yugoslavia. We trailed late in the first half of our game against Israel, but the tide turned when the refs got involved; luckily for us, they were calling fouls on Israel. At one point we shot seven straight free throws, and Tony Simms—one of the most athletic guys ever to wear the maple leaf—smashed down a dunk that looked as though he took off from the free-throw line. He then stole the ensuing inbounds pass and scored again. We were on our way to victory.

After the game, we checked the scores of the other games—we were second in our pool, while the Americans were first in theirs.

"We're playing Sir Charles and King Karl in the semifinal," Jack told us.

It went without saying that if we lost, the best we could do was bronze, and we hadn't spent our summer dodging mosquitos not to win gold. We were on edge leading up to the game. Jack sensed our excitement and nerves, so after one of our practices, he brought Cal, our team psychologist, into the dressing room.

"Playing the Americans in the semifinals is the best thing that could have happened to you," Cal said to us.

"How so?" I asked.

"Think about it," he said. "It's better to play them in the semifinal. They won't be as prepared as they would be in the final—they probably assume they'll be playing for gold."

That thought helped calm us, and on the morning of the game we were very loose. We knew what we needed to do. We went to the shootaround and walked through our offensive sets and defensive coverages—there were no last-minute strategies to implement. We barely got a sweat on. Billy had his boom box. We listened to "Sail On." We ate together. Then we rested in the dormitories until the game.

Cal was a big believer in visualization, in narrowing your focus and seeing in your mind exactly what you wanted to do, in the smallest detail possible. "If you can see it, you can do it," he always said.

Lying on my bed in the dormitory, I could see everything happening before I even took the floor. Every detail was already being played out in my imagination. The feel of my jersey against my skin, the lighting in the gym, the leather ball on my fingertips. I always found a way to believe in myself, to start a contest with confidence—justified or not—and sometimes that feeling is stronger than others. Sometimes it feels almost like destiny. This would be our time to win.

As I walked out to the floor for warm-ups, I had goose bumps. The gym was packed. More than ten thousand people had braved the mosquitos to come and watch. There was so much going on, but one guy by the free-throw line caught my eye. His sign said, "Miracle on wood." For me, that said it all.

The game itself seemed to unfold in slow motion. We were in the zone—that mental and physical state where we were at one with our performance. What we saw in our mind's eye, we were able to do out there on the floor in real time. By halftime, I had 21 points, and with every basket, a win seemed more and more possible. We started a smaller lineup than the Americans did—focused more on shooting and ball movement than on rebounding—and played at a fast pace, pressing the Americans and forcing turnovers. We could sense early that they were off their game. At one point, the United States picked up a foul for kicking one of our players, and a little later another of its players was ejected. We kept our cool even as the crowd was going nuts. In the second half, the Americans came at us with everything they had, but that was when our point guard, Eli Pasquale, was at his best. It seemed as though none of his shots could miss, and his passes found us through every gap. And on defence, anytime the United States tried to mount a comeback, he was there, diffusing the situation. The rest of us got a surge of energy from his play, and we didn't give an inch the rest of the game.

We won 85–77. We had beaten the United States on our home floor. It was a life-changing moment, but there was no time to celebrate. Our goal wasn't *only* to beat the United States; our goal was to win gold. We had to beat Yugoslavia in the finals, and our game with them in the preliminary round had not gone well.

They were the defending European champions, and they came to Edmonton with a team led by the Petrović brothers, who were renowned on the international stage. At that time, Dražen Petrović was a brilliant shooting guard on his way to becoming the NBA's first European superstar.

We were tired after the US match, but when we stepped onto the floor, the gym filled with cheering fans gave us the lift we needed. *There's nothing like playing at home*, I thought as I got ready for the tip-off.

We stormed out to the lead at the beginning, and everything we did seemed to work perfectly. By halftime, we were up by 19. In the dressing room, it was clear: the gold medal was ours to lose. I looked around the room at this band of brothers whom I'd spent the whole summer with.

"Guys, we may be tired, but we've got twenty minutes of work to do and the rest of the summer to relax," I said. "Stay locked in, focus on the process, and let's take this one play at a time."

The other guys all shouted their consent. I could almost feel the energy pulsing around the room. I looked around and saw the same determination in every guy's eyes—I knew we'd all go to the mat to win this game.

The second half of the game was like a coronation. Yugoslavia never mounted any kind of comeback. Between the energy from our home crowd and our lead, the Yugoslavians seemed discouraged. When the final buzzer sounded, it was pandemonium. I went to find some scissors to cut down the nets from both hoops. Eli made the first cut, then passed the scissors to me. The rest of the team followed—Bill, Karl Tilleman, Tony Simms, Danny Meagher, Howard Kelsey, Gerry Kazanowski, we all got a turn. We left the last cut for Jack. He was doing a television interview, but we dragged him away and lifted him onto our shoulders the way he had lifted us onto his—and would continue to do long after our careers were over, though we were too young to know that then.

When people ask me about the celebration, I joke, "Which day?" because the feeling of satisfaction and the sense of brotherhood continued long after that night. The next day I woke up still not quite believing what had happened, still not processing that the gold medal sitting there on the dresser in my dorm room at the University of Alberta was mine. Later that morning, I picked up a newspaper and opened it to the sports page to see a picture of the medal ceremony. In the photo, Howard is on the top of the podium, wearing his medal, and he's leaning down to let Sir Charles look at the gold that everyone had thought would belong to the Americans but for the first time was ours. I remember what popped into my mind was one of those Norman Rockwell paintings where a moment is captured and there are so many stories in it that the longer you look, the more you see. For me, the hope was that the best story was yet to be written.

CHAPTER 5

CHASING OLYMPIC GOLD

In the summer of 1984, we were on the verge of becoming Olympians. Just one more tournament in Toronto, and we would fly out to Los Angeles for the Olympic Games. Missing the 1980 Olympic Games in Moscow had been a tough lesson but a good one: there was no way I was taking this Olympics for granted. Not after years of late-night workouts, running stadium stairs with the SFU track team, and putting my NBA hopes—slim as they might have been— on the back burner.

As we rolled down the highways of southern Ontario, we knew our dream of winning a medal was well within reach. I remember throwing hamburger buns out of the driver's-side window of one of our team vans, trying to thread the needle and score a hit on one of my teammates sitting in the passenger side of the other van in the lane beside us. That was no easy feat at 120 kilometres per hour, but

I was feeling confident. Throwing buns and whatever other bits of scrap food we could find at one another might have been a weird way of showing it, but when teams are loose, goofy, and able to enjoy the moment, it's usually a sign that something good is on the way. And tearing down the highway, music blaring, food flying, we felt we were on the way to somewhere good. Somewhere great.

We weren't the exact group that had won gold in Edmonton. Stew Granger and Leo Rautins had finished their rookie seasons in the NBA and weren't eligible to play in the Olympics, and before we had headed to São Paolo, Brazil, for the qualifying tournament earlier that summer, we'd thought we might lose two of our best big men, Greg Wiltjer and Gerry Kazanowski. They were still under contract to their European clubs, but everything had gotten ironed out and we had gone to Brazil and simply romped. So often, when we played in South America, the games were close and the crowd or the conditions or the officiating came into play. But not this time. We were too good.

We won our first five games in five days by an average of 18 points each game. Three of the nine teams would advance to the Olympics. Puerto Rico was the only shoo-in, but even they couldn't touch us. Three of our starters—myself included—had four fouls, and with seven minutes left, it was a close, one-point game. But then we went on a tear, and we ended up winning by 14. We were playing a highly patient, structured brand of offense that frustrated our opponents, and defensively we were on a string, trusting one another.

After the win over Puerto Rico, my buddy Romel Raffin came up to me. He was the only other guy who had been on the team as long as I had.

"I can feel us gelling, Jay. We're coming together," he said. "We had that on that 1980 team, remember?"

I did remember. And Romel was right. We were the highest-scoring team in the tournament. We probably could have rolled through the event undefeated, but we had a mental letdown and stubbed our toes against Uruguay. Then it happened again when we played our host, Brazil. Even though we lost that last game, it raised our belief to another level. It had been a bar fight of a basketball game, but what else was new? The crowd was insane, which is always the case when you play a South American team on its home floor. There were 16,000 people there, and about 15,980 of them were pro-Brazil. We knew from our win in Edmonton how much a home crowd helps. I figure it's worth 10 points, at least, and we lost by 6.

We chose to see our defeat against Brazil in that environment as a positive, and we came home believing that in any other setting we could beat them. We believed we could beat almost anybody.

The next stop on our pre-Olympic tour was some summer basketball in New York City. That sounds nice and easy, but this was a Pro-Am league made up of NBA players keeping their games sharp in the off-season. It's a kind of basketball that's not as tightly controlled by coaching staff, but the intense level of athleticism was more consistent with what we would face against the Americans and the top European teams.

What I remember most from the trip isn't the basketball. It was Jack, a true-blue New Yorker, who took us on a journey through time as we visited the city. We couldn't go anywhere without his bumping into someone he knew—a hot dog vendor, the bellman at the hotel, or a cop on the beat. And if by chance he didn't know them, they recognized him, and we'd soon be introduced to some-body's brother's cousin from the neighbourhood. Jack was a socia-ble guy.

"I'm going to go for dinner. Anybody want to go?" he would ask each night.

The other guys would mumble something about resting, but I always went with Jack because I knew I would meet someone or do something new. That's one of the reasons I've been so lucky to be in the right places at the right times.

One night when we were in New York, Jack said, "We're having a team outing tonight. Be ready in the lobby of the hotel at seven p.m."

I was pumped. What did Jack have up his sleeve tonight? We headed down to the front entrance, some of us more eager than others, and there in front of the building was a row of seven Rolls-Royce limousines.

"What the hell?" we asked.

"They're for you," Jack said. "Get in. We're going to visit some-one I know."

We arrived at a beautiful building on Park Avenue and were ushered up to a penthouse apartment with floor-to-ceiling win-dows that overlooked Central Park. It was the home of one of New York's most successful fashion designers.

He introduced himself and then started talking about how he knew Jack. "I owe everything I have to this man because when I was in the tenth grade, he cut me from the basketball team."

I could hear the emotion in his voice. It wasn't anger or resentment—it was appreciation.

"When Jack cut me from the team, I had to go out and find my way." He smiled. "I started with a pair of socks, and once I sold the socks, I bought a shirt, and I sold that, too. That's how I built this empire. It was Jack Donohue who changed my life."

And Jack cut him! I thought as I looked around. *Holy shit. Look where he went.*

Then the designer took us out to eat at Mamma Leone's, a fancy Italian restaurant in the theatre district, one that cameoed in Billy Joel's song "Movin' Out." It was a crazy night, but it was par for the course with Jack. There was something about him that made people want to be with him, whether they were Olympic athletes or not.

We played our first few games, but we had one hiccup when Billy dunked over someone. He hung on to the rim to make sure he didn't get his legs taken out from under him on the landing, which would have been a good idea, except that the rim broke. Billy slammed to the floor, hit his head, and went into a seizure. Our team doctor, Andrew Pipe, tended to him while we waited for an ambulance, which seemed to take forever. After forty minutes, the paramedics finally arrived and took Billy to the hospital. He spent a couple of nights there, but thankfully, he was given a clean bill of health and was ready to play the rest of the summer.

After New York City, we had one more test, a mini-tournament in Toronto against Australia, Yugoslavia, and Italy—teams we would have to beat if we wanted to win that gold medal in LA. It was tough competition, but we were just as good on the floor as we were in the highway hamburger bun fights. We won comfortably over Australia, lost a game we probably should have won to Italy, and then beat Yugoslavia in the final game of round-robin play. Because of the point differential—Jack made sure to remind us of Romania again—we had to play Yugoslavia again, and that game was a war. We led by 11 early in the second quarter before they came back and tied the game with four seconds left on the clock. But we took control early in the overtime and won 99–97.

Jack was over the moon. "I don't get paid for overtime, guys," he joked. "But I'm happy that a game like that was the end of our Olympic preparation."

We were 16–3 that summer leading into the Olympics, with wins over every conceivable kind of opponent and back-to-back victories over Yugoslavia. As the captain, I wanted to make sure the team knew we were set. "We've worked very hard for this," I told the boys. "We have a good chance against anyone."

With that we were off to Los Angeles, where dreams are manufactured every day.

Olympic basketball is the lengthiest tournament in the summer Games. It starts on the first day and goes until the very last. We'd known for months that our first game was going to be the day after the opening ceremonies, and Jack was adamant that we would not be attending the march into the stadium.

"There's no way you're going to spend twelve hours standing in the hot sun the day before your first game," he said. "This is the Olympics. You've trained your whole life for this moment. If you wanted to march in a parade, you should have become a Shriner."

I would have loved to experience marching with the whole of Team Canada wearing our country's colours under our flag. But Jack was right, as always, and we skipped the ceremony. We did, however, get the full Olympic wardrobe. It was like sports Christmas. We had new tracksuits and T-shirts and very small, tight-fitting swimwear—Speedos, to be exact. Red and white with a little Canadian flag on the front. Did our swimmers Victor Davis and

Alex Baumann get basketball shoes? I don't think so, but we got bathing suits.

We thought the new swimwear was hilarious—Speedos don't fit basketball players the way they do swimmers. We had very little access to the fabulous Forum in Inglewood, California, where the basketball games were going on, so we trained in a suburban high school gym. There was no air-conditioning, and it could get pretty hot. Before one of our practices, guys were threatening to wear only their new Speedos for shootaround so that they could stay cool. Thankfully, the banana hammocks never made an appearance on the court.

The Games themselves presented their own challenge. We were so used to competing in far-off places where we had no one to rely on but one another. In Bucharest, we had been alone. In São Paolo, we had been alone. Even in Edmonton, it had been us against the mosquitos, our brotherhood against boredom. But the Los Angeles Olympics were something different. Friends and family—the people who made our dreams possible—were taking vacation time to come to the Games and share the moment with us. And we were dazzled by everything that LA had to offer. As soon as we were done with practice, *boom*, everybody was gone his own way. We would get together again at midnight curfew and exchange stories—*I went to a Dodgers game, I went and watched wrestling*. It was fun, but we were distracted.

Our point guard, Eli, had grown up in Sudbury and knew Alex Baumann, so we met up with him after his first event.

"Alex, how did the semifinal go?" I asked. The final, I knew, was that night.

"Not bad, I made a few mistakes and knew I would be a couple of tenths off my best time," he replied. "I'll set the record tonight."

I was blown away. "How can you possibly feel if you're off by a tenth of a second?"

He raised an eyebrow. "Jay, do you know before you shoot whether or not the ball is going in?"

He had a point, and Alex was true to his word—he set the world record that night.

We weren't as sharp. We were a couple of tenths off coming out the gate, too, maybe more. We were in a pool with Spain, the United States, France, China, and Uruguay. With only twelve teams total, the Olympic tournament is extremely exclusive, so any draw was difficult.

We kicked things off against Spain in a foul-filled game that almost disintegrated into a brawl several times—our kind of basketball, in other words. The only problem was that, collectively, we couldn't hit a free throw. Spain was called for thirty-eight fouls and we had twenty-nine, but we sank less than 65 percent of our free throws, and that killed us. We lost by a point, but we didn't have time to worry about it. We had an even greater challenge ahead; we were playing Michael Jordan the next day.

Michael was the number three pick in the NBA draft that summer, and I remember watching him hit the game-winning shot for North Carolina in the NCAA title game as a freshman in 1982. We had some personal history with him, too. We'd played against Jordan the summer before at the Pan Am Games in Carácas, Venezuela. It hadn't taken us long to figure out that he was unlike any other player. He was so quick and explosive—I'd never encountered that kind of athleticism—but it was the edge he played with that made him such a force on the court.

When we first played Jordan in Venezuela, we knew that if we were going to win, we would have to stop him. Or at least try to slow him down. Whenever the United States shot a free throw, my focus was on making sure Jordan couldn't get to the ball.

"If the rebound comes, you let the ball hit you in the back of the head, roll down your back off your ass, and someone else on the team will pick it up," Jack told me. "If you try to spin on him, he's so fast that he'll go past you and get the ball."

Every time we lined up, I would put my elbow on top of Michael's and lock arms so he couldn't get a good initial jump. When the ball went up, I was like an offensive lineman in football, facing him and trying to stay between him and the ball. I could tell Michael was getting a bit frustrated. *I must be doing my job*, I thought and kept at it. Elbow over top, elbow over top.

Still, we were down by 10 late in the fourth quarter, and we knew they were going to win. We were back in our end, lined up for the United States to shoot another pair of free throws. The first shot went up, and I locked up Michael's elbow, blocking him from getting the ball. It worked.

The next part is a bit fuzzy. I remember lining up again and placing my elbow over Michael's, but the next thing I knew, I was lying on my back with my teammates gathered around me.

"What day is it?" our trainer asked me.

"Tuesday?" *I guess I let go of Michael's arm a little bit too soon*, I thought as everything came back into focus. *He must have been a little more frustrated with me than I realized.*

My teammates filled me in on the rest. When I'd let Michael's elbow go, it had shot out—right into the side of my head. I had never been knocked unconscious before and haven't since. My claim to fame is that the only time I've been knocked out was by Michael Fucking Jordan. It was worth the headache.

Years later, I was at the Tournament of the Americas in Portland, Oregon, coaching Team Canada with the incomparable Ken Shields, when the US team, including Michael, entered the arena. He came up to me.

"Why are you not playing?" he asked me. At that time, he was on his way to becoming the most famous athlete in the world.

"I can't play. I'm old."

"Yeah, right," he said. "You could absolutely still play." He slapped my hand and headed out to the floor.

I heard laughter behind me and turned to see a security guard, whose face was a mask of disbelief. "You know Michael Jordan?" he asked. "Fuck me! How do *you* know Michael Jordan? That's Michael Jordan. Oh, my God, that was Michael Fucking Jordan!"

There was nothing that dramatic when we met Michael in the Olympics in the summer of 1984. The US basketball team was the talk of the Olympics, and a lot of that had to do with Michael. The Team USA we faced in Los Angeles was slightly different from the one we'd seen at the South American tournament. At the Olympics, there was no Sir Charles and no King Karl. Their coach, Bobby Knight, had cut them—two of the top fifty players in the NBA—in training camp. The team was so good, even without them, simply because they had Michael.

"We've beaten those jerseys before," I reminded the team before the game. "We can do it again."

"We only have to beat them once," Jack added.

But eight minutes into the game, we were trailing 22–6, and I was struggling. The United States put wave after wave of long, quick defenders on me—Michael, of course, but also Alvin Robertson, one of the original Toronto Raptors, and Vern Fleming, another athletic wing defender. All summer, Tony Simms—six foot six, rangy, and as athletic as anyone who has ever played for Canada—and I had been the go-to scorers, but we couldn't make our shots.

Jack called a time-out. "Settle down, guys. Don't let the game get away from you."

We tried, but we weren't letting the game get away from us—Michael was dragging it out of our hands. He had a couple of spectacular dunks, and at the half, we were down 43–28.

We made a little run in the second half, but Michael shut the door pretty quickly. Jack called a few more time-outs, but nothing worked. We lost 89–69.

As much as we wanted a win, we weren't too discouraged. We still had a chance to upset the United States in the medal round. If we were going to beat them once, we could do it there. Still, in order to even get the chance to face them again, we would need to win all of our next three games.

Basketball is a team game, and my role was to provide the offense. I felt the team members looking at me to create momentum by making plays and shots. This was the most important moment of my career, and I wasn't scoring. The pressure was weighing me down, but luckily we had a veteran group of players with enough shared experiences, good and bad, that we didn't panic.

"We've been in tough situations before," we assured one another. "And we've come out on top."

Jack also did his part to deflect attention from us onto him. The day after our game against the United States, he walked into practice wearing tight bright red polyester pants and a pink silk shirt—his outfit for our must-win game against China. We nearly collapsed our lungs, we were laughing so hard.

"Guys, relax," he said to us before the game that night. "It's just basketball. We've never lost to China before, and we aren't going to now."

By halftime we were up by 17. All twelve of us were playing and scoring, and Jack continued to keep things light. After a time-out, he tried to sit down and missed his chair, landing flat on his back. We all burst out laughing. We went on to win 120–79 and I scored 33 points, which gave me confidence that I was doing the right things.

As we walked back to the dressing room, Steve Konchalski, our assistant coach, said, "That win was just what the doctor ordered." He was absolutely right.

We didn't leave anything to chance in our next two games. We gave everything we had to beat Uruguay. And in our final round-robin game, against France, Jack left me in the game even after it was pretty much in the bag—he wanted to make sure that I had a good run and would enter the medal round with confidence. We finished 3–2 in the first round to enter a sudden-death quarterfinal with Italy, a veteran team that had beaten us by 2 points in Toronto the last time we had played.

"Win and we'll have a chance to play for the gold medal," Jack said. "Lose and we wait four more years."

"We're being tested," I said to the guys. "There are only two outcomes: triumph or disaster. If we stay on course, we're going to live to fight again. And we will stay on course."

We sure didn't make things easy for ourselves. Late in the first half, we were down by 11, and it wasn't looking good. But we'd been in worse spots in much worse places, and we pushed back, cutting the lead to 6 before the buzzer signaled halftime.

Back in the locker room, I looked at the faces of the guys around me and saw determination, not frustration. We'd been into battle together before, and this band of brothers was going to bring its best for the next twenty minutes.

Jack kept it simple and spoke from his big Irish New Yorker heart to ours. "Don't forget how hard you've worked to get here, boys," he said. "Leave it on the floor."

And we did. We seized the moment. We had been shooting 50 percent in the first half, which was pretty good, but we went out aggressively and improved to 60 percent. The Italians were the bigger team, but we attacked the basket with our speed and kept them in foul trouble all game. It was the most impressive effort I've been a part of with the national team. We won the game on the line, making thirteen more free throws than they did.

Joy was coursing through our veins as we ran toward each other after the final buzzer sounded, and outside our dressing room, we were like twelve-year-olds screaming at the top of our lungs, Jack included.

"That was the best game I've ever coached!" Jack yelled above the din. "You guys did it! You sucked it up!"

We didn't have long to let loose. We had to prepare for our next game and our chance to play for a medal, hopefully gold. To do that, though, we were going to have to go through Michael Jordan once again.

To beat the United States, we would need a scripted start. That was not a team we could play catch-up with, and we wouldn't be able to beat them by dominating the area around the hoop. Our only hope was to shoot well from the perimeter of the court and cross our fingers that Jordan and his entourage would struggle.

That was the plan, at least. But their defence was unstoppable. In the first half, we shot poorly, and they scored in the transition off our misses. In one stretch of more than four minutes, we scored just once in ten possessions. By halftime, news spread that US runner Carl Lewis had won gold in the 200-metre race. The crowd began to chant "USA, USA." The energy in the building was palpable, and it showed on the court. With sixteen minutes left in the game, the United States was ahead by 19 points.

I would love for this to be the part of the story where David toppled Goliath, where we kept loading our slingshot and took down perhaps the best US national team prior to the legendary Dream Team era of three consecutive Olympic gold medals. But not every story has a storybook ending. We needed to be perfect to beat the Americans, and we weren't.

Just like that, our dream of winning gold was over. We didn't wallow in our loss, though. We were disappointed not to be playing for gold, of course, but we still had an opportunity to play for bronze, and by the next day, our attention was entirely focused on that final game. We held on to the hope that we could still go home with a medal and that the last four years—or in my case, six years—would not have been in vain. We just had to beat Yugoslavia.

At that time, Yugoslavia was the premier power in European basketball, and it would remain so right up until the country broke apart in 1991. Everyone always said, "The United States invented basketball, but Yugoslavia perfected it." As a Canadian, I objected to the first part of that statement, but the second? That was hard to argue with. We knew we had our work cut out for us. Once again, we'd be going up against Dražen Dalipagić, who, at thirty-two, was already one of the top fifty basketball players in European history. The battles against Yugoslavia earlier that summer in Toronto were fresh in our minds, and I'm sure our win over them in Edmonton was fresh in theirs.

We entered the game confidently. At halftime, we trailed 44–48, but that wasn't unusual for us in this tournament. Dražen had scored 24 points, and Yugoslavia was using all of its guys to get him the ball. We did everything we could to stop him. We played man-to-man defence, we played zone. We played a combo of both—a box-and-one—on Dražen, but his teammates would run him off four or five screens just to get him the ball. Tony was our most talented defender, and even he couldn't handle him. At one point, Tony stripped the ball as Dražen was beginning his shooting motion, but Dražen grabbed it in midair, transferred it to his left hand, and made the shot anyway. Another time he was gathering to shoot and I slapped the ball three times, but he still made the shot.

We kept grinding, and in the second half, we slid into the lead by 2 points with seven and a half minutes left on the clock. Three minutes left, and we were still ahead. And then, impossibly, Dražen kicked things into another gear. We played a fantastic game, but we were dealing with a force of nature. The roll call of top Yugoslavian stars is a long one, and Dražen made the difference. He finished the game with 37 points, the tournament high, and announced his retirement from the national team immediately afterward.

Every win is a little different. Sometimes you steal one, and sometimes it's never in doubt. Sometimes you celebrate like soldiers home on leave, sometimes you slap hands and move on to the next one. Sometimes, depending on how you played and what your expectations were, you're angry that you won in spite of how you played, not because of it.

But losses are always the same. The sick feeling in your stomach. The helplessness. In the dressing room after the game, a sad, emotional fatigue settled over the room. It was like every other loss but magnified by ten. We were crushed. We had put years into this game and had fallen three minutes short.

We comforted ourselves with the knowledge that we were the fourth best team in the world, but all we could think about was how our team would never be the same again. In those situations, losing the game hurts, but losing the opportunity to play alongside your brothers hurts more. We would always have our friendships, forged by sweat and sacrifice, but we would never all play together again.

CHAPTER 6

THE IMPOSSIBLE DREAM

The weeks and months following the LA Olympics were a low point for me. Since 1978, I'd spent every minute of every day making decisions that in some way, shape, or form had prepared me for the Olympic Games.

Jack always taught me to write down what I wanted. "If you think about something, it might happen," he'd say. "But if you write it down and put it somewhere you can see it every day, the chances of it happening double."

But for the first time in my life, I had no goals. There were no lists to make. I had crossed off the number one item. I was only twenty-six and I was playing the best basketball of my life, but there was no obvious path forward. The next Olympic Games were four years away. What was I supposed to do in the meantime?

I had some downtime, so I returned home to Niagara for my

longest extended stay since I'd left for SFU. I tried to do normal, everyday people stuff. I spent a lot of time at a bar called Clancy's—basically Niagara Falls' version of Cheers—and hung out with my old buddies and my brother, Jeff. He had just finished four years of junior hockey with the Toronto Marlies and wasn't sure what he was going to do next, either. Between the two of us, we had a lot of time to kill. How much time? Well, so much that I took up fishing.

I'd never been a fan of fishing, but Jeff was really into it. "You should join me, Jay," he said one night. "It'll be fun."

It sounded like a good idea at the time, but the next morning, I regretted having let Jeff talk me into it. "It's frigging freezing out here," I complained as I tried to warm my hands in the car. "I can't see a thing."

"Don't worry. I know the best place."

He took me to a small spot in Port Dalhousie where all the old Italian guys went and waited for the fish to run. They were already crowding the edge of the pond, and I was anxious to get Jeff and me our own spot.

"There." I pointed to a place away from the crowd. "Let's go there."

"We can't. The stream's too low, and you can't cast. That's why everyone is over there," Jeff replied, gesturing to the men crowded on the other side of the water.

"We'll be fine." I didn't want to wait. I wanted to fish.

Jeff grudgingly followed me, and we got into position. There was a large tree overhead, so when I went to cast, I did so at an angle. The line went a good thirty-five feet. *Not bad for my first cast*, I thought. *Maybe there is something to this fishing thing.*

Right away, I felt a tug. "Jeff, I think I caught one! It's pulling pretty good." I started to reel in my line.

Jeff was horrified. "Jay! Cut the line! Cut the line!"

"No, I've got it, I've got it."

Little did I know that I had cast my line across all the other fishermen's lines and was reeling them in. The men started shouting from across the pond, wondering what was happening. That's when I realized I was ruining their morning of fishing.

"Cut your fucking line!" Jeff yelled again. "Cut the line!" Finally he reached up and did it himself.

"Whoops," I said.

Jeff rolled his eyes. "Let's get out of here."

That was the end of my fishing career, and I still had the problem of what to do with my spare time. Though I had a business degree, I'd never had a job. I had half-heartedly looked for one, but I wasn't that driven.

"You have to start working," my parents would tell me whenever they saw me on the living room couch.

"Why?" I would ask. "I don't even live here that much. I'll figure something out eventually."

That's when my mom would drill down on her main concern. "When are you going to get married and have kids?"

"Mom, I have kids," I'd say. "I just don't know where they are." It wasn't true, but it was fun to see how she reacted to my teasing.

"Don't you say that!" she'd say, covering her ears with her hands.

"Then stop asking me," I'd say.

Something had to change, and that's when Stan Stewardson, my old coach from SFU, called and asked if I would come out to the school to rally the troops for an alumni game during the preseason. I had nothing else to do, so I said yes. Then he asked me another question: "Have you ever thought about teaching?"

The bond between coaches and players runs deep. Sometimes coaches understand their players better than they understand themselves. Did Stan know I was floundering after the Olympics? I'm not sure, but it was clear that he hadn't stopped thinking about what might be best for me.

"I haven't, no," I replied. "I'm focused on the 1988 Olympics right now, but I haven't thought much beyond that. Whatever I do, I want it to be about basketball."

"Do you want to coach? If you get your degree in teaching, you can coach."

Coaching wasn't a foreign concept; some of the most influential people in my life were coaches. *And it's better than fishing*, I thought.

"You've got to do something," Stan said. "And we have a great teaching program here."

I wasn't in Burnaby for ten minutes before Stan laid out the details of his plan. "You're meeting this afternoon with the dean of the education program," he said.

"I am?" I asked.

"Yes. Your past grades are good enough that if you want, you can start classes at Christmas."

I was a little overwhelmed. "Oh, okay. Thanks."

But Stan wasn't done. "And, I want you to be my assistant coach."

My post-Olympic fog cleared pretty quickly after that.

Stan reappeared in my life at an important time and helped me shape my future in ways I wouldn't realize for years. He knew that my immediate plan was to go to the 1988 Olympics in Seoul, Korea, and that I still needed to compete. Both Stan and my instructors at teachers college were great at letting me pursue playing opportunities when they arose.

There was a long road ahead before the next Olympics, though. Canada's next major basketball competition was the World University Games in Kobe, Japan, in 1985. As the captain of the defending gold medal basketball team, I had the incredible honour of being the flag bearer and leading our country into the opening ceremonies.

The national team looked a bit different from our last time at the World University Games. Only six of us remained from the group that had finished fourth in 1984. We didn't make it to the gold medal round, but we made it to the bronze medal game against Bulgaria, where we closed a 10-point gap in the final two minutes to win third place. It was an amazing comeback and helped reenergize and focus the team. Winning a medal at the 1988 Games suddenly seemed like a realistic goal we could build toward.

The challenge for me over the next three years was to keep growing as a basketball player now that my university basketball days were over. It was clear to me that, at twenty-seven, making the NBA was no longer a realistic option, so I had to look elsewhere.

That left international basketball. My old teammate from the national team Howard Kelsey and I went to play in a Mexican professional league. Howard had played in Mexico the year before, and he was looking for some new players. Our team was based in Guadalajara. The money wasn't great, but the fact that we had a place to stay and were getting paid to play basketball made us feel rich in all of the important ways.

We lived in a hotel and ate every meal in the restaurant in the lobby. Guadalajara was massive by my standards, but I didn't have much of a chance to explore. I was there to play basketball, and with four games every week, there wasn't much time for anything else.

Because the city was so sprawling, the team gave us a car to drive to practices. Whenever we went to the gym, Howard would pay a kid a little money to watch the car while we were practicing. This system worked well for a time.

"Got any money on you?" Howard asked me one day.

I rummaged through my pockets. "No."

"Me neither." He turned to the kid outside our window. "Sorry."

That was a big mistake. A couple hours later, we came out of practice to find every nonessential thing stripped from the car. The dials on the radio, the knobs for the windows, everything. We had the key and the car still worked, so we drove it home. All for a nickel. We never forgot to bring money again.

We learned a lot about Mexico during the two seasons we played there. We often had long bus rides, sometimes up to seventeen hours, to get to games. When I got onto the bus for our first trip—more of a school bus than a coach—I saw an unfamiliar guy sitting up front.

"Who is that?" I asked the driver.

"He's our security guard."

Why would we need security? I wondered. My curiosity got the better of me, and I went to ask the guard.

He looked at me thoughtfully. "When we get on roads in the middle of northern Mexico, the banditos will jump out in front of the bus," he said in broken English. "The bus driver can't run them over. They'll have guns, and they'll take everything. If that happens, just give them everything."

I nodded, but inside I was thinking, *What have I gotten myself into?*

"I'll stay here as they come on the bus, but when they try to leave with all your stuff"—he paused and showed me his guns—"I'll shoot them and give you all your stuff back."

I couldn't sleep for the seventeen hours of the trip. Luckily, we never encountered any banditos.

Playing ball in Mexico was one of the wildest experiences of my career, but playing on an elite team kept my skills sharp. When the Mexican season ended in December, I went back to Vancouver, where I picked up coaching again and entered a year of teachers college. As if I weren't busy enough, I also started playing tournaments with a team called Brewster-Heights Packing, a powerhouse in the Amateur Athletics Union (AAU) in the United States.

When people hear the phrase "AAU basketball," they typically think of high school–aged players on the road to the NBA. But at the time, the AAU represented the highest level of competition for senior men's basketball outside of the pro game or NCAA Division 1. And Brewster-Heights Packing was very competitive, with a roster of former Division 1 and pro players. A massive apple-packing company based in Okanogan, Washington, sponsored the team. I spent almost every weekend driving down from Vancouver to Seattle to play with them or flying to meet the team at a tournament somewhere across the United States.

I'd often take Eli Pasquale, who was also looking for some good competition, with me. We'd get into Seattle on Friday night and sleep on our coach's floor for a couple of nights, spend the weekend practicing or playing a game, then drive back late Sunday night. I was all over the place.

Early on, some of the newer guys on the team would look at us skeptically whenever Eli and I rolled in.

"Don't fool yourself," the veterans told them. "These Canadian boys can play."

And we did. We won the national championship in 1985 and would go on to win two more in 1987 and 1988. It was while I was playing with the team that first year that I was offered my second pro contract.

We were in Colorado Springs for one of our league games, and before the game, one of the team officials let us know that the owner of a Turkish team was in the stands to scout the game. I put the thought out of my mind almost as soon as I heard it. There were too many things I was trying to get off the ground—coaching, teaching, and ultimately an Olympic gold medal. *This is not the time to be moving to Turkey to play basketball*, I thought.

I focused on the game, and I was on that night, shooting and passing well. Late in the game, I was at the foul line, about to take my first of two free throws, when someone in the crowd shouted out, "Jay Triano, do you want to come play in Turkey?"

"No," I called back, then made my shot. I looked over and saw the Turkish owner standing at his seat.

"I'll pay you forty thousand dollars!" he yelled after I sank my second shot.

I started running back on defence, but I made up my mind before I reached centre court. "I'm in!" I shouted.

The next weekend, I flew to Istanbul for a tour of the city and the team facilities. I was a bit skeptical at first; living in Turkey would be a big change. But the coach showed me how great the organization was, and by the time they showed me the contract, I was ready for the adventure. That September, I started playing for Fen-erbahçe, one of the most famous sports clubs in the world.

I immediately fell in love with Istanbul. The Bosphorus Strait divides the city into two parts, and historically, the waterway is the dividing line between Asia and Europe. I lived on the east side—the Asian side—of the city, but we practiced and played in the Euro-pean half. Every day, I would crowd onto one of the ferries that took me from one continent to the other.

The city and its people were among the friendliest I'd ever en-countered. Istanbul, thanks to its geography and history, was like the centre of the world. You could get any type of food. You saw people dressed in traditional clothing as much as you saw them sporting the most up-to-date European fashions. It was an exciting time to be living there.

Turkish basketball was just getting under way at the time, and we foreign players were treated like royalty. Along with my apart-ment, the team offered me a car, which was more than I could have asked for.

Of course, with the perks came the pressure to produce. I was a long way from home, and every time I looked in the mirror, I wondered what I was doing there. *You have a purpose, Jay*, I'd tell myself. *You're getting ready to play for Canada.* Even when I was thousands of kilometres away from home, my thoughts always re-turned to the courts in Canada and my dream of bringing home an Olympic gold.

The upcoming Games were particularly loaded with signifi-cance for me. Jack had announced that he wasn't going to seek a new contract with the national team after the next Olympics. I knew they would be my last Games as well. It was getting too hard to find places to play and stay active during the four years between the competitions. Real life was waiting for me. My personal life was changing, too. I had a serious girlfriend, Beth, whom I'd met at Simon Fraser when I was in teachers college, and we planned to get married after the Games. It seemed as though my coaching job at SFU would be taking more of my time in the seasons to come, too.

"Jay, I'm not going to coach here for much longer," Stan said. "I'll coach the season after the Olympics, but I'd like you to become my full-time assistant. Then, when I step aside, I want you to take my job as head coach."

"What will the administration think of that?" I asked.

"I've already talked to them, and they're on board. They want someone close to the program who can go into Ontario and recruit top players. With your connections and your reputation, we're confident you'll do great."

I was flattered that Stan had such confidence in my coaching abilities, and the job sounded perfect. It wasn't a lot of money, but it meant I could stay in basketball, which was what mattered most to me. I was also looking forward to sharing my knowledge of the game with a brand-new generation of players. I felt as though I were walking in the footsteps of some of my personal heroes: my high school coaches, Stan, and of course, Jack.

But before I stepped into that next chapter of my life, I still had some unfinished business. Canada did, too. This was our last dance.

We were gunning for our fourth straight Olympic appearance, and my time in Mexico and Turkey had kept me sharp. Plus, the introduction of the three-point line following the 1984 Games played right into my hands. I was a good shooter, but now I had something specific to focus on—a high-value skill. I had one goal: to become the best three-point shooter in the world.

The early results were promising. At the 1986 World Championships, our team performed as usual: we went 2–3 in pool play, with a chance to upset the favourites in the medal round. I was learning quickly how much of a weapon the deep ball could be. I made all five of my three-pointers in a win against Argentina, four in a win against New Zealand, and five more in a loss to Italy. It was that loss and another one to our old friends, Yugoslavia, that cost us a chance at a medal.

Our qualifying for the Los Angeles Games had unfolded nearly perfectly, but this time, every step was a grind. The pre-Olympic qualification tournament in 1987 was in Montevideo, Uruguay, and we got off on the wrong foot at the very start when Uruguay upset us in pool play. Things digressed from there, and we barely made the semifinals. We played Puerto Rico, blowing a 14-point lead to lose the game. That put us into the worst position possible in international basketball. If we wanted to have any chance of qualifying for the 1988 Games, we would need to win against Uruguay, the team that not only had already beaten us but had home court advantage.

The conditions didn't help. It was winter in South America, and the arena was ice cold. We called the building the freezer and the court the fridge. When we walked onto the floor for our do-or-die game, we felt like fresh meat. We warmed up but had to keep ducking the coins being tossed by the seventeen thousand Uruguayan fans in the upper deck. We had never felt so far from home.

Before the game, Jack asked us to write down on a piece of paper the people who believed we were going to qualify for Seoul. Most of us could have done it on a napkin. Even Canada Basketball—then Basketball Canada—was in the midst of cutting our funding. They didn't think we were going to qualify. It was us against the world.

We came out strong, but early in the game, John Hatch, one of the toughest guys I've ever played with, got hit in the head by a coin thrown from the crowd, and he started bleeding profusely. The doctors rushed onto the court, but John just stood there and began wiping the blood up and down his face and all over his arms.

"Bring it on, motherfuckers!" he roared at the crowd. It was like watching professional wrestling.

The doctors finally got him off the floor. They shaved his head and closed the wound with staples, and then he was back in the game, running around and diving for every loose ball. John's bravado triggered something inside all of us. I could feel my chest swell with pride in my teammates. It was twenty of us Canadians against seventeen thousand in the building, but at that point it could have been the entire world staring us down and I would have liked our chances. By halftime, we were leading, and we didn't let up. Early in the second half, the crowd began to realize what we already felt: Uruguay was going to lose. That's disappointing for any fan, but the Uruguay crowd was especially upset because their government had spent so much money on hosting the qualification tournament and now they were letting their chance to play in the Olympics slip away. The court filled with boos as the fans began to turn on their home team. It was absolute madness. Before the game was even over, Uruguay's head coach had to leave the building for his safety.

Once the win was on the board and we knew we were going to Seoul, we went nuts in the locker room.

"We're going to the Olympics!" everyone kept shouting, arms around one another as we bounced up and down.

"You guys have no idea!" I said to the new guys on the team, Wayne Yearwood, Dwight Walton, and Dave Turcotte. "It's the best thing ever. You're going to get a bag of clothes—Speedos for everyone!" I turned to Jack. "Maybe we'll even march in the opening ceremonies this time, eh?"

He laughed. "Schedules permitting, Jay."

Jack had always believed in us when no one else did. No one had expected us to qualify, so when we came back from Uruguay, there were no games, practices, travel, or accommodations planned. Jack was understandably frustrated. The years of dealing with a sports bureaucracy and funding issues were wearing on him.

"I go to meetings, and they spend the first two hours trying to agree on what day it is," he complained. "You can't run a program that way!"

Every decision Jack made was scrutinized, and the media felt he was too committed to the old guard. When they referenced me, Eli, or Hatch, it was as though we were going on fifty years old. Many other international teams were loaded with guys who were in their late twenties or early thirties, just like us. But somehow in Canada, that was a bad thing. When Jack decided to bring Romel Raffin back for his fourth Olympics, the critics focused on his age (thirty-four) rather than his experience and the unflappable defence skills that he brought to the team. Perhaps they were comparing us to the US team, which was still made up of mostly college-age players.

As we headed into the Games, we looked for inspiration in our new team anthem, "The Impossible Dream," a popular song from the Broadway musical *Man of La Mancha* about following a quest.

Again, it wasn't the typical pump-up song you would expect from a bunch of twenty- and thirty-something athletes. But we were trying to do the unexpected, so the message of striving for the impossible resonated deep within us.

The United States was still the team to beat in Seoul. Our best chance to silence the critics came in our round-robin game against the United States. That time, we made sure to throw the first punch against a roster that—Michael Jordan aside—we felt was more talented than the '84 team. Their team in Seoul featured Danny Manning and David Robinson—two number one picks—future Hall of Famer Mitch Richmond, and seven other players taken in the top fifteen of the NBA draft. Still, as talented as their athletes were, they had been together for only two months. We might not have been as athletic, but our eight years of playing for Jack leveled the odds.

Unlike in the '84 Games, we didn't let ourselves get overwhelmed. Before the United States scored its first basket, I hit a three-pointer in transition and Eli followed up with one of his own. By the second half, we'd pushed our lead to 50–42. My protégé at SFU Al Kristmanson was great, and his herky-jerky dribble-hesitation moves and runners off the glass gave the United States fits. He finished with 25 points.

I wish I could say I cleaned up, but after 8 points in the first half, I struggled to get clean looks at the net. Their rangy wing players and Robinson were protecting the rim too well. With nine minutes left, they took advantage of a few uncharacteristic turnovers and pushed ahead of us. The "USA, USA" chants started ringing out, but we weren't rattled. I hit another three and followed up with a pair of free throws to keep it tight. A few plays later, I got my hand on the ball as their point guard, Charles E. Smith, tried to drive to the net. Eli picked up the loose ball and found me on the break to put us within 4 points. There were two minutes left in the game.

The Americans began to stall, and we could sense an opening. But we turned it over one more time, and former Phoenix Suns star Dan Majerle (aka Thunder Dan) drained a deep three to give the United States the edge it needed to win.

At the final buzzer, we were heartbroken, not just because we had come within a few baskets of upsetting the United States but because we had already lost our opening game to Brazil and were now 0–2 in the tournament. Our margin of error for winning a medal was now razor thin.

We blew out Egypt in our next match—coincidentally on my birthday, which was nice—but then faltered against Spain. I was off my game, but our shooting guard Karl Tilleman wasn't. He exploded with one of the best shooting performances I have ever seen: 37 points, including ten of sixteen from three, in just twenty-six minutes. Still, it wasn't enough to beat the Spaniards, so we would have to win against China in our final round-robin game to advance to the quarterfinals. *We've done it before, we can do it again,* I thought.

In the second half, we were up by 12, but China pushed back. I knew that time was running out and the score was tight. A time-out was called, and I had a chance to look up at the scoreboard. We were tied with just twenty-six seconds left on the clock. We set up for the inbounds pass, and I got the ball and drove to the net, looking for a basket or a foul. I got neither.

But I knew Eli would be trailing me; that's what chemistry is, trusting that someone will be there for you when you need them. China's defence had collapsed close to the hoop when I drove in, so

I grabbed my rebound and flipped the ball to Eli on the perimeter. He leapt up and knocked down the game-winning three. It was just his fourth shot of the game, but it was never in doubt.

As with any tournament, our relief at making the quarterfinals was short-lived. With the win, we drew the top seed in the other pool: Yugoslavia. It had ended our medal hopes in LA, and that still stung.

In the dressing room before the quarterfinal, we played "The Impossible Dream" once again. We needed to beat Yugoslavia just once. It might take a miracle, but, as Jack used to say, "We don't believe in miracles, we count on them."

"Let's take the game to them, guys," I said, trying to rally everyone before the game. "We're going to fight them every step of the way."

We hung with them early and did a good job on Petrović all game, but it didn't matter. They had me bottled in, and I shot poorly. They were a team in every sense. Cut off one limb, and they seemed to grow another. Vlade Divac could orchestrate everything from the post. Toni Kukoč was a six-foot-eleven point guard. Stojko Vranković was a seven-footer who made the paint his own, defensively. We were down 40–26 at the half, and *then* Yugoslavia got hot, pouring in 55 points during the final twenty minutes. We lost 95–73. We lost to a better team.

Yugoslavia went on to lose to the USSR in the gold medal final—the last time the Soviets were together before the fall of the Berlin Wall. The United States, with all its talent, could manage only bronze, a disappointment that precipitated the Dream Team era, NBA players competing in the Olympics, and the explosion of basketball globally. The Seoul Olympics changed the game of basketball forever, and it was an honour to be on the front lines, navigating the chaos, trying to play better, and, most of all, fighting to survive.

For eleven years, I'd been chasing an Olympic medal. I wept in the dressing room after the game, thinking how I would never stand on an Olympic podium or wear my country's colours as an athlete. We hadn't been good enough—*I* hadn't been good enough—and I would never be in the fight with my brothers again. That was the end of the line for Jack and me. I thought it marked the last time I would ever have any connection to the national team. After everything Jack had given us, I wished we'd been able to give him more.

CHAPTER 7

STEPPING BEHIND THE BENCH

My decision to retire as a player was fairly easy; that was one of the advantages of playing basketball internationally in the era I did. There weren't a lot of opportunities outside of international competitions, and without the national team, the effort it took to stay ready to compete at the highest level was tiresome. Driving down to Seattle every weekend and sleeping in my car or on the floor at my coach's house had been exciting in my twenties but was less than ideal now that I was in my early thirties. Besides, once you've gone to the Olympics, playing in a men's league feels like going backward. At least that's what it felt like to me. I'd been fortunate to live my boyhood dream for half of my life, but that chapter was ending and another was beginning. I was excited about the new path opening up in front of me. I just had to take the first steps.

Stan helped me with that. My friends were well into their careers, getting married, buying homes, and starting to make decent money. I was engaged, but the rest of the things on that list seemed beyond my reach.

"Let's buy a house," Stan said to me when I first started coaching with him. It was something he offered a lot of former players; it was his way of helping them get a head start in life.

"Stan, I'm broke. I can't buy a house," I replied.

But he had a plan. "You're a first-time buyer, so you'll get a grant for five thousand dollars. I'll match that," he said nonchalantly. "That makes ten thousand. We can get a good mortgage. It'll be good for you—I'll show you how it's done. Let's start looking."

Outside basketball, real estate was Stan's area of expertise. He owned Basketball House, where we'd had all those epic parties back in my university days. He had bought several run-down houses and hired us as his demolition and landscaping crew, fixing up the places so he could flip them.

"Get rid of that hedge. Do these floors. Drywall here. Paint it up." Even as a contractor, Stan coached us.

Together Stan and I found a house smack-dab on the way up the mountain to SFU—perfect for student housing. We got a $50,000 mortgage and bought the place for $60,000. We turned the garage into two bedrooms and rented the house to five of our players to cover the mortgage payments. As soon as everything was running smoothly, Stan said, "You're all set now. Buy me out."

Just like that, I was no longer a broke, about-to-retire Olympic athlete but a full-time assistant coach, property owner, and landlord. Thanks to Stan looking out for me, when Beth and I got married, we had a home to live in. My parents were delighted that I was settling down and about to start a family.

My post-Olympic life was coming together, but I still had a lot to learn about coaching—namely, that it's harder than it looks. No one thinks he can teach grade twelve math better than the math teacher, but for some reason we often think of coaching as a job that anyone can do. Maybe it's because so many of us have been coached or feel we know so much about the sport. Though I had spent enough time watching Stan and Jack to know there was more to the job than calling time-outs and ranting at referees, in 1989 I still wasn't ready to be a head coach.

The teams at SFU were competitive, and we performed well, but things didn't always go smoothly. I was still figuring out how to best serve the players around me as a coach rather than a teammate. I expected every player to be like me and love the sport more than anything else. When I realized that not everyone felt the same way, I tried to adjust and see things from their perspective, but it was hard. I'd spent so long understanding and appreciating the game on my own terms that it was hard to reframe my thinking. I didn't always have the answers for those challenges. Like most young coaches, I probably did a disservice to a lot of my players. So much of the learning curve in coaching takes place on the job, and it takes time to grow into the role. I had to learn to analyze what had made my former teammates and me successful if I was going to be able to translate that to my new players.

I fell back on the lessons about patience, determination, and commitment that my own coaches had instilled in me. Jack was never far from my mind. I would often hear his voice in my head, and without thinking, out of my mouth would come the same phrases and philosophies, minus the Brooklyn accent.

I wasn't just coaching players; I was coaching myself. On the back of my clipboard, I wrote a question: "How can I be a better coach, a better husband, and a better father?" If I wrote it down, my chances of success would be much greater—that's what Jack had taught me.

Slowly I began to get into a coaching routine, and I realized that my role was about so much more than communicating technical details. Jack wasn't a Canadian Basketball Hall of Famer and the only Canadian coach in the FIBA (International Basketball Federation) Hall of Fame because he was an Xs-and-Os guy who had reinvented how to play the game. Yes, he knew his stuff. I use some of his drills and offensive elements from the 1970s and 1980s to this day. But his coaching was more about relationships and chemistry and learning how to persevere together.

Often, as I was getting ready for a game, an image of Jack would come to mind—this intense, funny New Yorker, always wearing grey Bike brand shorts, dark glasses, and a Canada Basketball T-shirt that half the time didn't cover his belly. To many, Jack probably looked like a caricature. But he could get grown men to run through walls for him. He knew how to be fun and still get his message across.

When you become a coach yourself, everyone who's ever coached you becomes a part of you. They're there in the background of every practice and every game, subtly guiding your choices and decisions. I could feel Jack's influence every time I stepped behind the bench, and I wanted to embody the values he'd instilled in me. He would always say, "You can only be a great basketball player for so long, but you can be a great person for the rest of your life." He was relentlessly positive and believed that if we fought for one another, we could handle any kind of pressure.

That, more than any technical element, was what I wanted to

bring to my coaching. Luckily, it was the easiest lesson to communicate, and it wasn't long until our opponents knew that if they were going to beat SFU, they would have to be ready to fight for every inch of wood—literally. We gained such a reputation that the football team used to come to our games because they never knew when a hockey-style fight would break out.

The foundation of any successful team is trust. It might not be in any coaching textbook, but it's the stuff that matters. And in that area, I followed the mentors who had come before me: Jack, Terry, Stan. I was aware that my players had lives outside of basketball, and I recognized that their whole person mattered. I made it clear that if they gave everything they had when they were on the court, I'd help them any way I could off of it.

I hadn't been coaching for long when Electronic Arts, a video game developer based in Burnaby, reached out to me about creating a basketball game. The company was just starting to produce more sports video games. I wasn't sure what I could do, but I said I would help.

"We'd like scouting reports on all the NBA teams," the rep said. "We want the teams to run their own plays by default. In other words, we want the Bulls to do what the Bulls would do under Phil Jackson."

"I'm not in the NBA," I said. "The reports are going to take some work, but I'm in."

I started scouting, watching and rewatching every game I could get my hands on, and writing up detailed reports. It was an unconventional but invaluable education.

"This is unbelievable!" the rep said when I presented my findings. "We just need one more thing."

"Sure."

"We need someone to rate all the players. Can you help us?"

"Yeah, I think so." The wheels were already turning. *What better way to evaluate the NBA than to have a bunch of video game–loving basketball players give their opinions?* I thought.

I starting picking the brains of the guys on the team during road trips. I drove the van, so my manager would read off the names of the NBA players and all nine players would rate them. We'd take the average and I'd present that to the people at EA. They loved it. I don't think many people realized that the earliest ratings in EA games were done by a bunch of guys from SFU in a van. It was a riot.

That was the beginning of a strong partnership between our program and Electronic Arts. Pretty soon, the company was even offering the players summer jobs.

"How many positions do you have?" I asked the rep during one of our meetings.

"As many as you can help us fill."

"You might get all twelve players," I said. "What would they do?"

"They would test the game, tell us what's right and what's wrong."

Not a bad way to spend the summer, I thought. Eight or nine guys started at EA that summer, and five of them went on to work for the company full-time after they finished playing for me. One of my players—Sean O'Brien—ended up being a key employee.

Granted, helping guys get a summer job playing video games wasn't exactly like Stan helping me get into the real estate market or Jack taking me all over the world for competitions. But it was important to me to follow in their tradition—to look out for my players in ways that were bigger than basketball and that might benefit them after they finished playing. *It's about the person, not just the player*, I thought.

I would discover that sometimes that philosophy can work against you. A big part of my job at SFU was recruiting, which I don't think any coach truly enjoys. We work our asses off to tell an eighteen-year-old how great he can be, and then, when he gets to school, we spend the first year letting him know that he's not that great yet. But it remains an essential part of the job. You need to identify the most promising players for your program and make sure they understand why your school would be the best place for them to reach their potential. It was a new challenge every time.

I remember going to Ottawa and getting four starters who won the Ontario championships that year. I remember sitting in the living room with Peter Guarasci in Niagara Falls. His mom cried at SFU's offer because she was scared her son was going to leave home, meet a girl, and settle down on the other side of the country. Which was exactly what happened. But I'm getting ahead of myself.

My most important recruit was the one that got away: Steve Nash.

The first time I saw Steve was in Victoria in the summer of 1989. The national team was training at the University of Victoria, and I had taken the ferry over to watch them train and visit with some of the guys. I was always recruiting, so while I was there, I watched a summer men's league game. That's when I noticed a shifty kid beating guys off the dribble and finishing strong with his left hand.

"Who's the left-handed kid?" I asked the guy next to me.

"What left-handed kid?" he said. "That's Steve Nash. He's right-handed."

What? I thought. *He's playing so confidently with his weak hand. And he's only in high school.*

I put Steve on my recruiting list right away, but I wasn't the only one. He was quickly developing a big reputation within BC basketball, and the more I watched him, the more I realized that he was a special player. The way he ran point could make an entire program.

I had to have him on my team. I knew that I would have to do a little extra to make sure Steve knew that I was interested in him as a person and would support him in everything, not just basketball. I attended his basketball games, as other interested coaches did, but I also went to his soccer games and stood beside his dad, John. When Steve's team won the BC high school basketball championship in 1992, I got a photograph of him with the freshly cut net around his neck, holding the MVP award, and had it blown up into a poster and delivered to his house. Such things weren't considered illegal recruiting gifts back then.

Steve was ambitious, and he wanted to play at the Division 1 level. I knew that US schools were interested, but they were slow to realize how talented he was, so I thought I had a shot to get him into SFU. Late in Steve's senior season, it was coming down to the wire between us and the University of Santa Clara in California, and he came over for a recruiting visit. We spent the day together, and I showed him the campus, the gym, and the court. We were clicking, but I could tell the decision was tearing him up.

At the end of the day, I took him to the Tsawwassen ferry to catch the boat back home to Victoria. It was a stormy day, the winds were up, and the ferry was delayed. I didn't feel right just leaving him there, so I waited with him. Even though he hadn't committed to

SFU or anyone else, the pressure was off. We started talking person to person, rather than coach to recruit.

"If you were me," Steve started, "what would you do?"

I was tempted to sell him one last time on SFU, promise him all the playing time he could ever want, warn him about how easy it is to get lost at a Division 1 school. But that wasn't who I was. Stan had never coached me like that. Jack had never coached me like that.

"Steve, you have to do what your heart is telling you to do," I said. "You're a really talented player, and I think if you go to the States, you'll do really well. I'd love to have you at SFU, and if things don't work out at Santa Clara, I'll always have a spot for you on my team."

He looked relieved. "Thanks, Jay, that means a lot."

"No problem, Steve." I replied confidently. "Besides, I'm going to coach the national team one day, and you're going to be my best player." *Dream big dreams, right, Jack?*

•

Big things were happening in the world of basketball in 1995. The NBA was expanding into Canada and establishing two teams: the Grizzlies in Vancouver and the Raptors in Toronto. The arrival of the Grizzlies was a game changer for BC basketball, but other than feeling excited about the NBA coming to my city, I didn't think much about it.

I was happy at SFU and was interested in moving up and taking on the role of athletics director, which I figured I could do in addition to my coaching. Beth and I had three young kids—Courtney was five years old by then, Jessica was three, and our youngest,

Dustin, had just turned one. And although Vancouver real estate prices weren't as high as they are today, life in the city was getting expensive, so we were looking forward to the salary bump a new job would bring. I'd been through two formal interviews, and the school was on the cusp of making its decision when I got a phone call from Stu Jackson, the president of the Vancouver Grizzlies.

I had met Stu through my good friend Steve Frost, who had moved from head of media relations at SFU to a similar role with the Vancouver Canucks and Grizzlies. Frosty had organized a press conference to introduce Stu to the basketball community, including me.

"Are you thinking of giving up coaching?" Stu asked me over the phone.

How did he know? Before I could ask, he answered my question. "I saw your name in the paper for the athletics director job."

"Oh, right," I replied. "I'm still going to coach. I figure I'll do both jobs for a year or two, then decide if I want to just be the athletic director."

"If you're considering stepping away from coaching, I want to talk to you."

I was still waiting to hear back about the athletics job. *Can't hurt to talk*, I thought. We arranged to meet a few days later.

"How much are you making coaching?" Stu asked when we got together.

I told him.

"I'll pay you the same to be the director of community relations for the Grizzlies," he said. "We need someone closely aligned with the local basketball scene who can help cement the bond between the club and the community and help grow the game."

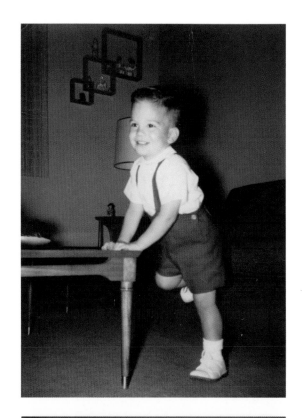

Me as a young
boy at our
family home
in Tillsonburg.
*Courtesy of Triano
family*

Whenever I wasn't shooting hoops in our driveway at home, you could find me at the baseball diamond. This team won the Canadian Championships in 1974. I'm in the very middle of the back row. *Courtesy of Triano family*

Friday night games at my high school, A.N. Myer, felt like *Friday Night Lights*.

Terry was a constant inspiration in the days I got to know him at SFU. From hanging out at his dance party fundraisers to watching him training for his Marathon of Hope, I learned how to live by the values he embodied.

From the moment I first saw the Canadian national team play, I wanted to play at Simon Fraser University—they had put more players on the national team than any other school at the time. In 1977, I finally had the chance to pull on the SFU jersey.

I tried out for both the Los Angeles Lakers and the Utah Jazz after I was drafted into the NBA. The experience of playing against such high-calibre players gave me a lot more confidence when I rejoined the Canadian national team.

When we beat the US on our home court at the 1983 World University Games, it was life-changing. After we beat Yugoslavia to take home the gold, we put Jack on our shoulders to cut down the net. *United Press Canada Limited*

Basketball has allowed me to travel and live all over the world, from Canada to Turkey to Mexico. In 1985, I was honoured to carry the Canadian flag as I led all Canadian athletes in the opening ceremonies for the World University Games in Kobe, Japan. *Athlete Information Bureau*

The 1988 Olympics in Seoul, South Korea, were my last playing with Team Canada. They also marked the end of an era—in future Olympics, NBA players would be allowed to compete, precipitating the USA Dream Team and the explosion of basketball globally. © *1988 Canadian Olympic Committee/S. Grant*

LEFT: When I started coaching, I often heard Jack's Brooklyn accent in my mind delivering one lesson or another about patience, determination, and commitment. *The Canadian Press/Gary Hershorn*

BELOW: When we went to the Sydney Olympics in 2000, the team gave it everything they could, but we fell short of our expectations. We went 5–2 but lost the wrong game. It was a tough journey, but I knew that one day, we'd be back. *© 2000 Canadian Olympic Committee*

When I took over as head coach of the Raptors in 2008, I became the first Canadian-born (and the first non-American) head coach in the NBA. My goal was to help the athletes around me become not just great players, but great people, just like Jack had taught me.

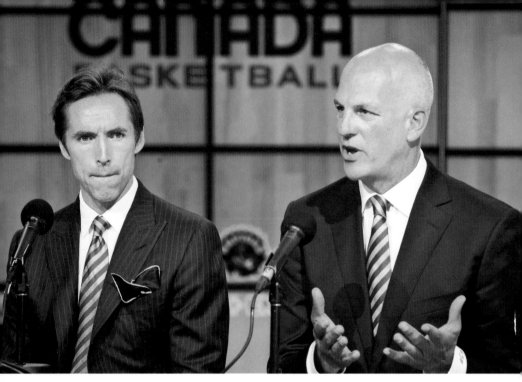

When Steve Nash asked me to come back and coach the national team for a second time, I couldn't say no. *David Cooper/Getty Images*

I'm still dreaming big dreams for our basketball teams. All I want is to bring a medal home for Canada. *Photo courtesy of Canada Basketball*

I didn't have any direct experience in community relations, but the more Stu explained the job, the more it sounded as though it was right up my alley. Plus, it was hard not to get excited about being attached to an NBA team.

"The basketball scene is already well developed here in the high schools and universities, so we wouldn't be starting from scratch," I said.

"Great. Say, have you ever tried broadcasting?"

I didn't think this was the time to mention my colour analyst work playing imaginary games of one-on-one against Bob McAdoo in my driveway in Niagara Falls as a kid. I did have some real experience with broadcasting from my time reporting on the Victoria Cougars for UVIC campus radio station prior to the 1984 Olympics. But I decided to keep that quiet. It wasn't as though I was looking to be a hockey broadcaster—I had just wanted to go the Cougars games for free.

"Not really." I said to Stu.

"We have an exhibition game coming up. You could try it out, and if it works out, you can do radio for us, too. We pay a thousand dollars a game."

I did the math in my head. *There are eighty-two games . . . that's $82,000 on top of my regular salary. And I'll be working for the NBA in my own city.*

"I'm in!" I said, trying to sound eager but not desperate. The NBA was the highest level of basketball, and as much as I loved coaching at SFU, working for the NBA was a dream opportunity that I couldn't pass up.

But first things first: I had to prove I could do a decent job analyzing an NBA game on radio. It was trial by fire, but I had the best first responder I could have hoped for in Don Poier, the Grizzlies' play-by-play announcer. An experienced broadcaster, Don had most recently called NCAA basketball and football in Seattle. If he had any problem being paired with a rookie who had been to only a handful of NBA games, he didn't show it.

"Don't worry about a thing, kid," Don said, patting my knee before our first game. "I'll teach you the ropes."

And he did. He would begin the commentary: "Greg Anthony drives baseline, pulls up for jump shot." Then he'd give me a hand signal when it was my turn to talk.

"Great shot! His feet were ready." I'd continue until Don gave another signal that he was ready to pick up the play-by-play again. He kept doing that: throwing it to me and pulling it back in.

"I like your energy, Jay!" he told me after the first game ended.

I was buzzing as I left the arena that night. I was excited that I'd gotten to sit in the front row of an NBA game, and I loved nothing more than talking basketball. I couldn't wait to get back for the next game.

During that preseason, Chris Hebb, the head of broadcasting for Orca Bay Sports and Entertainment and the owner of the Grizzlies and the Canucks, came and sat courtside with Don and me as we did our broadcast. I must have done all right, because after the game, I was hired. I was no longer a basketball coach at my alma mater. Now I was an NBA broadcaster with a side in community relations.

I still had a lot to learn, though. My job was twofold: to educate the first-time listener who was new to the NBA in Canada while still entertaining the hard-core fan who already knew the game. Thankfully, Don continued to mentor me. I wouldn't have been able to do it without him—Don was one of those people who changed my life. He missed a couple of games, but we worked just about every game together. When the Grizzlies moved to Memphis in 2001, he went with them. I was sad to see him leave Vancouver, and I was sadder still when, four years later, he died of a heart attack in his hotel room after saying good night on the phone to his wife, Barb. The media room at the FedExForum in Memphis was named after him.

I was sitting on the sidelines of the Grizzlies games, and a big part of me wanted to be closer to the action. I was still too close to playing and coaching. I hated to lose—I'm competitive to my very core—and the Grizzlies lost a lot. Three hundred fifty-nine games out of 460, to be exact.

Part of the reason for the Grizzlies' struggles was that they hadn't been allowed to have a top-five pick for their first draft in 1995. That meant they had missed out on Kevin Garnett and took Bryant "Big Country" Reeves. During the draft, I'd kept an eye out to see if Steve's name might pop up—I wondered if Stu would snatch him up. He didn't, and the next year, Steve went fifteenth overall while the Grizzlies took Shareef "Reef" Abdur-Rahim. Reef would go on to be an amazing player, but at that time, I couldn't help imagining what an impact a local kid like Steve would have had on our standing in the BC community.

The losses started to get to me. In the Grizzlies' second season, we travelled to LA for an away game and were headed to the hotel on the bus. We had just lost an afternoon game in Vancouver, and I was pissed. Probably just as much as the players and coaching staff who were on the bus behind us.

"Jaybird, are we going to go for a run?" Debbie Butt, the media relations director, asked. She was trying to convince me to train for a marathon.

"No, I'm going to go get fucking drunk," I replied. At that moment, it was dead silent on the bus. I could have been on a megaphone, it was so quiet. Everyone heard my frustration, and I could feel my face going red. I might have been only broadcasting the games, but I was emotionally invested in the team. Still, I knew that radio commentators weren't meant to be voicing their opinions for everyone to hear after a loss.

The Grizzlies head coach, Brian Hill, turned around and stared at me for a moment. "I'm with you," he said. "Five minutes in the lobby."

That was a turning point for me. Brian saw that I cared about the team and that I was competitive, not just a local guy doing the broadcasts and going through the motions. From then on, my involvement in the team changed.

"Jay, we're going to go for dinner at Carabas at seven o'clock," Brian said a few weeks later. "You're more than welcome to join us."

Every night after that, I went to dinner with the coaches. Did we talk tactics? Did we talk strategy? No, we told stories about the game. The NBA was a long way from growing up in Niagara Falls, playing on Burnaby Mountain, or even competing in the Olympics. Immersing myself in the world and learning the language was an amazing education.

The funny thing about the NBA is that it's the most professional environment you can imagine, yet basketball is still just a game that depends on the whims of athletes who are so talented that they can get away with things no one else could. A big part of my community relations role was getting players to do things they didn't necessarily want to do. Most of them were good about visiting schools, hospitals, or community centres once they got there. Sometimes, though, the problem was simply getting there.

Debbie had a great way with the players. She could tell when they were nervous and knew how to coach them through their talks.

"You've got this," she said before one presentation. "You're going to thank the indigenous people whose land we're on and then talk about the environment and youth basketball. You can remember these three things. Get out there." She was great, and I often used her method of focusing on three key teaching points to organize my own presentations.

Even though I was the broadcaster, I travelled with the team, so I knew the players' schedules, specifically when they would have a day off and be available for a school visit.

"Let's get this visit knocked off, then the rest of the day is yours," I'd cajole them.

Being there every day helped give me an in with the players, but it was still hit-and-miss.

"I'm coming by your house at eleven thirty a.m. tomorrow to take you to the Abbotsford event," I said to Anthony Peeler one day. "Cool?"

"Cool," he said.

The next day, I parked outside the security gate of his house and not a soul was stirring. After a minute or two, I tried calling him, but he didn't answer. I looked at the clock anxiously. Stu hated it when the guys missed appearances.

Screw it, I thought and climbed the security gate. I could hear music coming from the house, so I banged on the door. Nothing. I looked up to the security camera.

"AP, we have to go. I know you can see me, man."

I checked my watch again. We were going to be late. I called the event coordinator and explained the situation.

"You have to get him here," he said. "We have three thousand people lined up."

Damn it! I looked around wildly for an idea. That's when I saw a beautiful Range Rover parked in the driveway. If there is one thing NBA players love more than basketball, it's their cars. I walked over and put my foot on the bumper, setting off the alarm.

Within seconds Anthony came running out of the house. "What the hell is going on?"

"AP, we have to be in Abbotsford in an hour."

"Oh shit, man."

"We have to go right now."

He hopped into the car and immediately fell asleep. He slept the entire way as though he'd never slept before. *This is going to be a disaster*, I thought.

When we got to the event, AP woke up, and he was on. For two hours, he talked with everyone, sat for pictures, signed autographs. It was the best event we'd ever had. Then we got into the car and he slept the whole way home.

There were a few shenanigans like that, but for the most part, being around the players taught me more about coaching.

One time we were on our way back from a game, and as I walked past Shareef on the plane, I noticed that he was quieter than usual. I could tell that the losses were getting to him. He'd signed a big contract and was putting up good offensive numbers, but the team wasn't going anywhere.

"Are you all right, Shareef?" I asked.

"Actually, do you have a minute to talk?" he asked.

"Sure," I said, sitting beside him. "What's up?"

"I know you coached a little bit," he said quietly. "I know you know the game. Can you tell me what I need to do to get better?"

"I don't know if I can, Reef," I said. "I'm the team broadcaster. You have coaches that are here to help you."

"I make so much money that they're afraid to tell me something critical. I just want to know what I need to do to improve."

I felt for Reef, but I didn't want to go behind anyone's back.

"What do you see?" he asked again.

I chatted with him about the game but refrained from giving actual coaching advice. For the most part, the players all care about the game. They want to be talked to, they want to be coached. They want to improve. A big part of coaching is honesty: sometimes you have to say things a player doesn't necessarily want to hear, because if you don't, you're selling him short as a coach. The key, I've learned, is to make sure the criticism comes from a place of love and trust. Luckily, I'd had someone on the road to do the same for me.

In my first year with the Grizzlies, I had a lot of time on my hands, so I did my fair share of drinking after losses and enjoying my per diem at restaurants in each city we went to. It was fun, but it definitely wasn't sustainable. By the end of that first season, I was out of shape and miserable.

"Jaybird, you look like shit," Debbie said to me one day. "Next year, you and I are going to train for a race."

Debbie got me to enter a 10K. After that, I signed up for the Vancouver Marathon the following spring. I'd wanted to try a marathon ever since I'd watched Terry run his Marathon of Hope. *If Terry could run a marathon every day, I can do one marathon*, I told myself. I trained like crazy, and I finished in 3:36, which was fine, given that I hadn't really had a specific goal for my first race. When I crossed the finish line, I was overcome by a mixture of relief and excitement. Finishing the marathon was one of my greatest personal accomplishments at that time, albeit a thoroughly humbling one.

Running was just what I needed. It scratched that itch I had for competition. When I was playing or coaching, it had been easy to stay disciplined because there had always been a game to get ready for. Marathon training instilled that in me again. *You have to earn your success*, I told myself whenever I didn't feel like training. Then I'd go out to do hills, intervals, and speed work.

As an athlete, I wanted to hit the proverbial wall and feel that fatigue so that I could move beyond it. I was determined to push myself harder. So I signed up for the Victoria Marathon, which boasted a much more difficult terrain than Vancouver. The day of the race, I went out fast, and everything was good until the five-mile mark. Then, out of nowhere, my right leg felt as though there were a knife in it. Every step I took, I felt a stab in my calf. I tried changing the way I ran, but nothing worked. I stumbled on, but when I saw the marker for one mile to the finish, I smashed into the wall.

All I could think was *I can't finish*. I took a step. Pain. Another. Pain. Then I had an epiphany. *This is what you wanted, Jay. You wanted the pain. You wanted the struggle. This is your chance.*

I knew that what I was feeling was nothing compared to what Terry had gone through, and he had never quit, whether he was pushing his wheelchair up that mountain in Burnaby or running on the road. He could have run forever—only cancer had stopped him in Thunder Bay.

What are you going to do, Jay? I started sprinting. Somehow I fought through the pain to find an extra gear. I finished the race with a time of 3:18, almost twenty minutes faster than my first one. The high I felt was incredible and filled a void I wasn't even aware I'd had.

With that second race, I had officially caught the running bug. I began to organize my routine around my training. For the rest of my time with the Grizzlies, my favourite days were the ones when we had a home game in Vancouver. I'd drive straight to Stanley Park after waking up and run the 10K around the park—it didn't matter if it was freezing cold or pouring rain—then drive to the arena, take a steam, and work on whatever community outreach the team had planned for the day. I'd call the seven o'clock broadcast, and then I'd head straight home.

It was an amazing time. But the itch didn't go away. The radio broadcaster who brooded over losses on the team bus was really an ex-player turned coach who needed a purpose and a team. I thought back to the note on my clipboard: "How can I be a better coach, a better husband, and a better father?"

I kept a close eye on the national basketball program. A lot of the players I had recruited—or tried to—were playing on the team, including Steve, Peter Guarasci, and Greg Newton. The team had failed to qualify for the Olympics in 1992, when the United States had won gold with its first "Dream Team" of NBA players—in the aftermath of the 1988 Olympics, the FIBA had ruled that NBA players could compete in the Olympics. Canada fell short again in 1996, and again the United States walked away with the gold medal. The international game was growing, but Canada was trailing behind. We had fallen far from the standing Jack had worked so hard to earn.

In the fall of 1998, Art Rutledge and John Mills from Canada

Basketball invited me to dinner in Vancouver. I had a feeling that the team would be undergoing some changes. I'd bumped into a few players who had hinted that morale wasn't great, and it seemed that the team was looking for a new coach.

"We need you, Jay," one of them said. "It's your time."

I thought about the idea of coaching the national team. How could I not? It was an incredible honour, one that, if they offered it, I knew I couldn't refuse. I was just forty years old, and the only coaching I'd done was six fairly unremarkable seasons at SFU. I wasn't the obvious candidate. I worried about the extra time away from my family, too. Was the timing right?

At dinner, Art got right down to it: "We want you to come coach the national team."

I looked at my beer, mulling over the dream offer to follow in Jack's footsteps and coach the program that had shaped my life. Despite my initial hesitations, I realized there was only one answer.

"Yes," I said. "Let's do it."

"Fantastic!"

"On one condition. I don't want the job unless it's going to be for six years." The 2000 Olympics were less than a year away, and I didn't see us qualifying. We would need to build toward 2004 and that would take time, but I was all in. I was back.

CHAPTER 8

THE ROAD TO SYDNEY

There was so little time to pull things together. I was still working with the Grizzlies, so most of the national team preparation took place during the summer. Thankfully, the Grizzlies allowed us to train in their facility in Richmond, British Columbia, so I didn't have to travel far.

Our best chance to return to the Olympics would come in 2004, but that didn't mean we could give up on the 2000 Games in Sydney. There were a lot of players, Steve included, who were hungry for the competition and didn't want to count themselves out, even if the rest of the world did. Only two teams would qualify from the Americas, and the Dream Team would be one. Canada was no one's favourite to be the other.

I had to start from scratch, and I needed help. In international basketball, you're only as good as your manager. The manager is the person who coordinates travel and makes sure that players from all over the country have what they need so that the team can maximize those precious few days of training camp. I immediately thought of Troy Wenzel, the Grizzlies' trainer and travelling secretary, but he was committed to the Grizzlies for the NBA summer league.

"They won't let me out of that," he said. "But Jon Lee, our visiting locker room guy, teaches at Richmond High, and he works his ass off."

I knew who Jon was; I had seen him around the arena. So before I went on air to call a Grizzlies game in early April, I asked him over to my community relations office.

"Jon, I'm going to be coaching the national team," I said. "I've heard really good things about you. Would you like to be our manager?"

I couldn't read his face, and when he turned and took a couple of steps toward the door, I thought, *That didn't go as planned.*

But then Jon turned around. "It would be the greatest honour of my life," he said with tears in his eyes.

I knew exactly what he meant.

The only way for Canada to succeed in international basketball was to have a team completely committed to the crest on the front of the jersey. Once I had selfless players who loved playing for their country as much as I had, I wanted to bring them to NBA-calibre play. Instead of drinking beer after games and practices, we would break down the video of the game and review it the next morning. I had to find players who would be willing to put in the work if we were even going to qualify for the Sydney Olympics.

We had fifteen guys in the training camp that summer, and I

needed to get that number down to twelve, then find some games for them to play. Canada Basketball, as usual, had little money to spare, but the Australians were willing to pay for us to come to Sydney in the summer of 1999 to give their national team, the mighty Boomers, some games and test out the Olympics facilities. It wasn't an ideal travel time for us, but the positives outweighed the negatives. I figured we could use the trip to get used to the jet leg and gauge how long it would take us to adapt. We'd also be able to get our sightseeing out of the way, ensuring that when we returned to Sydney for the Olympics the next year, we would be entirely focused on the competition.

Unfortunately, Steve wouldn't be travelling to Australia with us. He was coming off a tough year with the Dallas Mavericks—he was battling a bunch of nagging injuries and had played only forty games. The fans in Dallas had started turning on him, making him the scapegoat for the team's misfortunes. Every time he touched the ball—which was a lot given that he was a point guard—the crowd would boo him. One of those games happened to be the first one that Steve's brother, Martin, went to see him play in the NBA. Steve kept looking over to where Martin was sitting and saw that he was laughing his ass off, which helped Steve put things in perspective. Still, given the year he'd had, the Mavericks weren't comfortable having Steve play for Canada, and he needed time to get healthy, so we forged ahead without him the first part of that summer.

Shortly before our trip, I still had to cut three players. In any coaching position, cutting players is the hardest thing to do, but when it comes to cutting players from the national team, it's even worse. If a player is cut from the national team a year out from the Olympics, chances are he'll never play for Canada at any Olympic

Games. It's the end of the road. I drafted a list of three players and called each of them into my office, one by one.

The first two cuts were tough on me. Guys had been in camp working and preparing for the chance to represent Canada. It's never easy. I always try to do it just before a practice so that they can slip out and we have plane tickets ready for them. I learned from Jack that it doesn't help anyone to have guys say good-bye to everyone. He wanted the guys who made it to feel good. They have just trained with the others, and they feel bad for their friends who got cut. So Jack never wanted anyone who'd just made the national team to feel sad. When you get cut it's tough, but we still have to build our team by moving forward. Everyone knows that we can take only twelve, so the players know there are going to be cuts. The first two went okay. I am sympathetic, and it hurts. I am the one who takes their dream away. I had one more to go to get to our twelve.

Then Shawn Swords walked in.

Everyone loved Shawn Swords, including me. He'd grow up in Ottawa playing hockey and had gone all the way to the juniors before switching his focus exclusively to basketball in university. It had made him a bit of a late bloomer, but he'd carried over the toughness from hockey into hoops. I loved his tough play, but there just weren't enough spots; I had to let him go.

Shawn sat down, and I started my spiel.

"Listen, Shawn, you've played really well these past two weeks. You're a great teammate, you hustle on defence, and you do everything that we ask you to do. But I can only take twelve guys on this trip, so I'm sorry, but I've got to let you go."

As I said the words, I realized I couldn't do it. All I could think of was how, twenty years ago, Jack had looked at his roster and seen some long-term potential in me, a player who was definitely ranked low on the roster. But Jack had cared about what kind of teammate I was going to be. Would I support the guys, or would I pout? Would I push them in practice, or would I be too caught up in my own frustration? I realized that Shawn was exactly that guy. No one competed harder. No one cared more about his teammates.

Before Shawn could even respond, I said, "You know what? Never mind. I'll see you tomorrow. You're not cut."

Shawn was clearly bewildered; he was at a loss for words. *He must think I'm crazy*, I thought.

Then I thought of the twelve available jersey numbers—they ran from four to fifteen. "By the way, you're going to have to wear a jersey that has a zero on it or no number."

"If it has 'Canada' on it, I don't care," he replied.

I'd made the right choice.

After Shawn left, I went back to the rest of the coaching staff.

"How did the cuts go?" one of them asked.

"I couldn't do it," I said.

"What do you mean? We leave tomorrow. We don't have enough room for thirteen guys."

"I know. But I just feel that Shawn brings a competitive spirit we're going to need."

The other coaches exchanged looks, but they seemed to understand what I was saying. We talked about how we would manage the logistics. I knew that taking Shawn was the right choice for the team, but I knew I was putting the rest of the staff into a tough place. I was incredibly grateful when one of the assistants graciously offered to stay behind so that we could take the extra player.

Our Australia trip was a tour of five cities, and we started off with an exhibition game against New Zealand. Given the long flight and time change, it wasn't surprising that our first game went badly, but as a coach, I couldn't let the players make excuses. I was trying to figure out how mad to be when Jon asked me if he could speak to the team first. *Couldn't he wait until I rehashed the game with them before he reminded them of some travel itinerary detail?* I thought, but there was something in his eyes, so I said, "Go ahead."

In the dressing room after the game, Jon looked at each player.

"First of all," he started, "I hate that we lost. But I don't give a shit." He picked up a sweaty jersey lying on the floor. "This jersey here, it says 'Canada,'" he said with emotion. "It should never touch the floor. I put a table right there. When you take your jersey off, you put it neatly on the table. It should never hit the floor. This is who we represent."

I didn't have much to say after that. The room was silent. The thought of the game was gone as the bigger picture of what we were representing dawned on the team.

I was lucky to have Jon; he lived the values that I wanted our team to have and helped set the tone for how I would coach. Despite our loss, I felt our tour had started on the best note possible.

Still, as much as I believed in our potential, we weren't brimming with high-end international talent, and we didn't have the cohesiveness I had experienced with Jack. To make up for that, I wanted to establish a hard-nosed style of play where we controlled the tempo, the clock, and the ball. That strategy didn't make for the prettiest basketball, but I believed it would be effective. There was a thirty-second shot clock, and we wanted to use all of it, moving the ball from side to side to side. That strategy worked as well as I could have hoped. We still lost two of our first three games, but the scores were low and were all very close. We were building our identity, which very quickly became "pissed-off underdog."

There was a good reason the guys were pissed off. As we flew from city to city, our limited budget meant we were in economy while the Australians were up front in first class. At the promotion banquets, we listened to speakers talk ad nauseam about Australia's hopes to contend for a medal the following summer, how our team "might" be in Sydney "if" we qualified. All of that fueled our fire, which boiled over in fights during a couple of games.

The headlines across the country said it all: "Basket Brawl—Aussies, Canadians Fight Again." The Australian officials even met with me to see if I might get my players to tone things down. "This behaviour isn't promoting the Olympics the way we want to," one official said.

But if we didn't play with an edge, we weren't good. The team lightened up in the fourth game, and we lost by 20 points.

"Did you think we could beat this team without a fight? Just because we had a couple of close games?" I shouted in the dressing room after the game. "You're wrong. We've kept it close because of how hard we're playing—we can't lose that."

The room was quiet other than the sound of my rising voice. "I hope you realize now that if you want to have a chance at the Olympics, you have to play my way. Who will fucking play the way that I want?" I asked.

Everyone in the room raised a hand.

"You, you, you, you, and you are starting," I said, pointing blindly. "Our last game is at Sydney Super Dome, the same place we're going to play during the Olympics, assuming we can get our shit together and qualify. Get out of here, get some rest, and be ready to roll tomorrow."

One by one, the players left the room without saying a word, and I finally started to cool down.

I turned to Jon. "Who did I point to?"

He sighed. "Coach, you don't want to know."

"No, really?"

"It's not good." He gave me the list, which was mostly our subs who hadn't played a whole lot yet, including Shawn, number 00. He'd barely played all trip. His biggest contribution had been getting kicked out for fighting in game three, but after that big speech, I had to start him.

At the game the next day, Shawn came out of the gate running— he was a maniac on defence and executed the game plan perfectly on offense, cutting, moving, reversing the ball. We started the game with a 9–0 lead. We were winning. Australia called a time-out, but it didn't matter. We kept rolling and beat them by 20 points, playing our way, our game. And Shawn? He finished with nine points, nine rebounds, and nine assists. Just shy of a triple double.

It was the perfect way to end our trip, and the flight home was a little sweeter because of it. I already knew that the first guy on our team was going to be Steve, but in Australia, I figured out, just as importantly, that our twelfth guy was going to be Shawn. Now I just had to worry about finding the other ten and molding them into a team that could qualify and compete at the Olympics for the first time since 1988. Those exhibition games had given me an idea of who would play on that team; most of the guys who had travelled with me would return the next year. But more than that, the trip gave the team something we could all share: an identity.

•

In July 1999, Steve was back, and we were feeling good about the qualifiers as we touched down in the scorching hot city of San Juan, Puerto Rico. The good vibes carried onto the court, too. At the end of the preliminary round, we were 5–2. We'd even had a huge win over an emerging Argentinean team that included the electric wing named Manu Ginóbili, along with several other players who would go on to form the core of Argentina's golden generation.

As the clock was winding down in the game against Argentina, we were up by five points. Rowan Barrett, one of our guards, was dribbling the ball up the court slowly, trying to run out the clock. But I remembered how points had been the tiebreaker for us in 1981, and I wasn't about to take any chances.

"Score!" I yelled at Rowan.

Rowan looked at me as though I were crazy, but I repeated the instruction. He took off down the court and scored an easy layup just as the buzzer went. I ran to the scorer's table to make sure the refs had counted the final bucket.

The next game, we were blown out by the United States, but considering that its roster included some of the greatest players in history—Kevin Garnett, Tim Duncan, Jason Kidd, and Gary Payton—we didn't feel too badly. Our only other loss in the round-robin was to the home team in front of their adoring, crazed fans. There may be no place in the Western Hemisphere that loves basketball more than Puerto Rico. The island nation of 3 million has its own league—the BSN, or Baloncesto Superior Nacional—and loves nothing more than to support its national team. The atmosphere at Roberto Clemente Coliseum was an incredible reminder of how wild international basketball is and that the crowd is as big a factor as the five players on the floor. There was no coin throwing as in Uruguay, but flags waved and horns blew, and the fans had special cheers for every kind of play.

After we lost to Puerto Rico, we rehashed the game in the dressing room.

"When we came here, our goal was to finish second or third in the preliminary rounds. We're in second place, so good work," I said, looking around at the disappointed but determined faces. "Tonight was exactly what we needed. We got a taste of how crazy the crowd is, and you guys handled it really well. We didn't get the win, but we stuck together and we battled."

Steve spoke up. "Guys, if we play Puerto Rico again, we're not going to let them beat us twice."

That's leadership. As coaches, we get a lot of credit for leadership when things go well and blame when they don't. What many fail to realize is that the best teams are led by the players. When I played for Jack, he certainly set the tone, but more than anything, he empowered Eli, Hatch, and me to raise our own voices. That was my strategy for the 2000 national team. I was their guide, but it was their journey.

Only the two finalists from the tournament would qualify for the Olympics. Everyone conceded that the Dream Team would win the pool play—which it did—so the best route to the finals was to avoid whatever semifinal the United States was in and win the other one. That meant we would have to finish second or third, not fourth, in the pool.

When the round-robin finished, we were tied with Argentina and Puerto Rico. We all had identical records. Once again, it all came down to points. It turned out that Rowan's layup was the difference maker. We'd clinched second place. That meant we would avoid playing the United States in the semis, but our reward was playing the home team on its home court—again. It was like in Uruguay in 1988, except instead of the fridge, we were heading into the frying pan. Luckily, we had the right guy doing the cooking: Steve Nash.

Steve is a rare person in a lot of ways, but one of his trademarks is his unselfishness. It's unusual that any athlete with his kind of ability would use every fiber of his being to make others better, but Steve did. On the court, he would work as hard as possible to get easy shots for other guys. Off the court, you would never know he was an NBA star who had just signed a $36 million contract. He had a roommate on the road; he paid for upgraded seats for his taller teammates, but he flew coach; he'd take guys out for lunch on his own dime. More than anything else, though, he kept things fun. As intense as the qualifying tournament was, it didn't stop him from dragging the group to the beach in the evenings and playing a game of 500-up with a soccer ball he'd brought with him.

But Steve was as serious as a storm cloud heading into our semifinal against Puerto Rico. After we walked through our game plan, he asked me, "Are we good? Is there anything you need from me?"

"We're good, but I don't know if we can score enough points," I said. "I think we need you to score at least twenty-five."

In our first eight games, Steve had done whatever we needed, but the emphasis had been on "we." The team. In our win over Cuba, he had played thirty-seven minutes and helped the guys get their shots off with nine assists, but he had scored only 2 points himself. He couldn't have been happier. Against Uruguay, our fourth game in four days, the guys were dragging a little, and he put up 21 points, five assists, and six rebounds. Whatever we needed, he delivered. Against Puerto Rico, we needed him to be the most dangerous player on the floor.

"Okay," he replied, giving me a look that I could take to the bank.

Steve knew that our first job was to reduce the power of the ten thousand flag-waving, chanting, singing fans, which he did by putting up a quick 15 points in the first half to give us a 6-point lead. As we headed back to the locker room at halftime, I turned to Steve. "The first five minutes after halftime will be crucial," I told him. "Command those, and we'll create doubt in the minds of their players and their crowd. Let them get back into it, and we'll have a lion to tame without the benefit of a whip."

The message sunk in—after the break, Steve dropped a pair of threes, right on cue, and by midway through the second half, we were up by 19. I played Shawn for one possession as a defensive substitute, and he made a steal and scored a layup in the space of five seconds.

But Puerto Rico wasn't about to let us go without a fight. They pushed back and got the score difference to within single digits, but then they got into foul trouble. Sherman Hamilton, one of our guards, knocked down eleven of twelve free throws. Puerto Rico couldn't recover, and before long, the final buzzer sounded. We had won. I had asked Steve for 25 points, and he'd given me 26, along with eight rebounds and four assists. We had slid into second place. We were going to Sydney.

We went crazy in the dressing room afterward, hugging and pouring water all over one another. The celebration and singing continued on the bus all the way back to the hotel. When we got back, I headed straight to my room, where I took calls as part of a media press conference. When I was done, I went back to the hotel lobby. The players mobbed me as soon as I walked out of the elevator. We laughed and dreamed and drank the evening away.

The next day, it was back to business as we got ready for our game in the finals against the United States. We put up a fight, but the United States' talent was too overpowering, and we fell short. It didn't dull our excitement, though—we knew the real competition was many months away, in Sydney. Also, after the finals, Steve was named the tournament MVP. I was thrilled for both him and the team. I couldn't help but think back to when I had been watching Steve play high school basketball in Victoria, hoping to recruit him to SFU. Just as I'd predicted that day waiting for the ferry, I was now his coach and he was my best player. I couldn't believe how far we'd come.

Coaching is about shaping lives and helping people's dreams come true, and as I looked at the happy faces in the locker room and thought about what was in store for them, I was overjoyed. They had given everything, despite the fact that no one had believed in them. There wasn't a single reporter from Canada in Puerto Rico, presumably because no one wanted to spend the money to cover a team that wasn't expected to qualify for the Olympics. We simply played for one another with one goal—a team goal—driving us. As we headed back to the hotel on the bus, the sound of all twelve players and the support staff singing "O Canada" at the top of their lungs was better than any medal I had ever won. Our anthem never sounded so bad or so incredibly good.

In the lead-up to the Games, I had to confirm the final roster for the team, and there were two big question marks. The first was Rick

Fox. Rick had played for Canada at the 1994 World Championships, but not since then. A nine-year NBA veteran, he was currently playing for the Lakers, who were coming off an NBA championship win. He was interested in coming back for the Olympics, but he wasn't sure if he'd be available. The other unknown factor was Jamaal Magloire, a senior at the University of Kentucky and a projected first-round pick in June. He was incredibly skilled, but it was hard to get ahold of him, and when I did, I wasn't sure if he wanted to be part of the team or not, as he was still forging his career in the NBA.

I was in a tough spot. My obligation was to put together the best team I possibly could, and I thought a pro like Rick and a talent like Jamaal would help. But how could I look past the group of guys who had put their lives on hold to be part of the team with no guarantees that they would end up on the final roster? Pete Guarasci and Shawn Swords had both just gotten married and left for training camp right after their honeymoons. Rowan Barrett was about to become a father, and the baby was due only weeks before we were scheduled to leave for Australia.

I kept returning to Jack's view on team building, that the twelve best players don't necessarily make the best team. We were on a mission, and I wanted only those who would be all in on the journey.

There were logistical hurdles, too. The next time the media asked about the roster, we were in Montreal for a three-game exhibition series against Brazil. I made the announcement. "Magloire and Fox are out," I said to the media. "They're not available when we need them."

That night, we lost a close game to Brazil, but there was a fight. Greg Newton dunked, and a Brazilian player hit him twice, once as he was hanging on the rim and again after he dropped to the ground. Our benches emptied. Greg was ejected for fighting, as was Shawn, who had jumped in to help. When I saw their fire on the floor, I was glad they were going to be around during the fight for the Olympic podium. They embodied the spirit of the team that Jack had always talked about.

We had no idea if we could win a medal, but we knew we could compete because we had an incredible brotherhood of players. Guys like Rowan and Steve had been in our junior program since they were teenagers. We were a young team by international standards, but we had put in the time together, and bonds like that can't be easily replicated.

When we arrived at the Olympic Village, so many memories came flooding back to me. Experience is that kind of teacher. Being an Olympian is an incredible honour, but the feeling that I might have left the tiniest crumb on the table during the 1984 LA Olympics had never completely faded away. As a coach, I wanted the team members to make every sacrifice so that they would never have to wonder if they had done everything they could to make the most of this precious moment. We had done all our sightseeing on our previous trip to Australia—walked the Sydney Harbour Bridge, toured the opera house, gone to the beach. So in our last meeting before we left, we walked through what obstacles we might face at the Games and how we could deal with them. We decided to bunker down in the village and leave only for practices and games. The whole team bought into the plan.

Big Todd MacCulloch put his hand up. "The Olympics were going to be part of my honeymoon, but I'm going to tell my wife I'll see her after the Games are over."

"I've got a bunch of family coming," Steve added. "But I'm going to be hanging with you guys."

And that's what we did. We ate our meals as a group, six guys on one side of the table facing the other six. In their spare time, they played cards or music (some guys had brought guitars). But the most hilarious way they spent their time was playing a special version of the board game Risk. In the players' version, strategy didn't matter—they would all just gang up on whatever country they were playing the next day. Only once they'd crushed that country would they play the game properly.

Just in case anyone was thinking of breaking the pact, David Cox, our sports psychologist, went on a condom rant. He'd read that the Olympic Village was supplied with ten thousand condoms and that at most Games they were gone within the first couple of days. So, on our way back from our first practice, he got up in front of the guys and waved around a copy of the newspaper article he'd read.

"I can't imagine training my whole life for the Olympics just to spend all my time chasing some girls from another country that I'd never see again," he said. "You can get laid the rest of your life. Don't waste your time on it for these two weeks."

The players listened and our focus was good, even if we felt out of our depth in the tournament. We never talked about winning or losing or medals or podiums. We talked about preparation and focus and making sure we were on time for buses and engaged while watching video recaps.

We were in a group with Australia, Spain, Yugoslavia, Angola, and Russia. Of the six teams in the pool, we were ranked fifth, ahead of only Angola. If everything went according to plan, our best-case scenario was a fourth-place finish and a quarterfinal matchup against the first-place team in the other pool, which was almost certainly going to be the United States. The stakes were high.

As luck would have it, our first game was against Australia. The tension in the locker room was palpable. The moment we'd been working toward since they had whooped us last summer was at hand. *But they've never played us with Steve running the show*, I thought.

"Smile, guys," I said as we got ready to head out onto the court. "Enjoy this. We're at the fucking Olympics."

We knew that the first five minutes were going to be critical— just as they had been against Puerto Rico in San Juan—and we wanted to come out flying. Sure enough, Steve found Michael Meeks for a couple of open threes to kick things off, but then the game quickly got away from us. Aussie Andrew Gaze, the country's flag bearer and a five-time Olympian, scored an early 12 points for a quick lead of 20–9. The crowd was unstoppable. In honour of Canada they were singing all kinds of Christmas songs, such as "Andrew Gaze walks on water, fa-la-la-la, la-la-la-la" and "Walking in a Winter Wonderland." When they were stumped, they shouted a simple "Aussie, Aussie, Aussie, oy, oy, oy."

We eventually made up some ground, and by the half, we trailed only 51–48. In the third quarter, we took control of the game with a 15–4 run that was capped off when Gaze knocked Steve down with an elbow and Steve threw a fifty-foot pass from his knees to Meeks for a layup. The Aussies and their fans were rattled. A year earlier, we'd been their practice fodder. Now we were beating them opening night at their Olympics. Steve finished with 15 points and fifteen assists, leading us to our first win of the Games.

"Nash had fifteen assists in an international basketball game," Gaze said after the game. "I've never seen that before."

Something special was happening, and we could feel it. Beating Australia wasn't just a big upset; it opened our path to a medal. "Our guys always believed in themselves," I said to the media afterward. "Maybe now the rest of the country can believe in us, too."

Our second game was against Angola, and we expected to win. The only problem was that we had an early game time, 9:30 a.m. The team always met and had a meal four hours before we played; that was the optimal time to get our nutrition. But if we did that here, we'd have to get up at 5 a.m. I wasn't sure what to do, but luckily, I met someone who did.

The team was a big fan of the US tennis player Todd Martin. We'd watched his epic five-set match at the US Open in Hong Kong even though we'd been jet-lagged and the match had gone on until one in the morning. Our sports psychologist, David Cox, knew Todd, who was apparently a big fan of ours, and David introduced us while we were waiting for a bus outside the village.

"It's so good to meet you guys," Todd said after shaking our hands. "The whole village was cheering for you to knock off Australia. What's your next game?"

"We're playing Angola at nine thirty in the morning, which is a difficult time for us because we have a pregame routine," I said.

"I know exactly what you mean," he said. "I used to have these nine a.m. games at Wimbledon, and I'd have to get up at four a.m. for my five-hour prematch rituals. Never mess with your routine. Time doesn't matter."

I noticed that the players were listening to Todd intently, so I decided to get their opinion.

"Are we doing the five a.m. wake-up call?" I asked the team at our next meeting.

"That's our routine, Coach," they said. "We're sticking with it."

We got up at 5 a.m., ate together, and went through our game plan. As we rolled out of the athletes' village three hours later, we passed the Angolan team, who'd just woken up and were picking at food they'd gotten on the way out the door. We blew them out of the water in that game, taking us to 2–0 in the pool.

In between games, the other coaches and I spent every spare minute in my room at the village, where we had written break-downs of every opponent in Sharpie on brown wrapping paper tacked to the walls. From my time with the Grizzlies, I knew that having good video breakdowns was a huge advantage. Gary Schmidt, the Grizzlies' video coordinator, worked for us night and day—he knew every play and was relentless in his preparation. And Mike Katz, a basketball savant who was my number one assistant, had been scouting our opposition for weeks. In the days before our next game against Spain, we rewatched the footage of its team, and that's when I noticed that their centres didn't like to run. *Our bigs love to run*, I thought. *Steve will hit them with passes all day long.*

The game was practically scripted, and Spain had no lines. Meeks finished a perfect eight of eight and made all his free throws, and Guarasci was five of seven. We knocked out Spain and became the talk of the tournament. Even the Canadian media covering the Olympics started to buzz about us.

We still had Russia and Yugoslavia to play, and there was no getting around the fact that they were the best teams in our pool. When we took the floor against Russia, we knew we'd have to be at our best, and even then, we might not get the win. Unfortunately, we weren't at our best. We shot just 33 percent—half of what we had been shooting coming into the game—and the game turned into a blowout, with Russia winning 77–59.

It was a tough loss. We had one more game against Yugoslavia, and if we lost it, we would end up in a three-way tie in the pool with Yugoslavia and Russia. Since we'd lost to Russia by such a large margin, though, the tiebreaking formula—that pesky points system—might not be in our favour. And it turned out that some people figured a loss to Yugoslavia was a given.

As I was walking off the floor after the Russia game, a FIBA official stopped me. "Jay, I need to explain the tiebreaker."

"What tiebreaker?"

"You are three-two, Russia is three-two, and Australia is three-two."

"We're not three-two," I said, thinking he'd just made a mistake.

"You play Yugoslavia," he said knowingly. "You could be three-two."

"But we're not fucking three-two," I repeated.

"I want to explain . . . you play *Yugoslavia*."

"We're not fucking three-two!" I said once more, then stormed away toward the locker room, where the guys were waiting.

The team was on edge in the locker room, and I could see the nervousness in their faces when I walked in. I realized that I was visibly ticked off and they probably figured I was going to yell at them because they had played poorly against the Russians. I paced around the room, trying to figure out what I was going to say.

"I'm sorry I'm late," I started. "Do you know where I was? I got stopped outside because a FIBA official said we were three-two."

"We're three-one," someone said.

"Exactly. He said we're three-two because we're playing Yugo-slavia in two days, and they have already got us down for a loss. They don't think we can win."

From all over the room, guys uttered, "What the fuck?"

That was all I had to say to motivate them. They got dressed, marched out, and got onto the bus. For the next two days, they were as mad as I was. It was perfect.

The first part of our game against Yugoslavia went as expected. Yugoslavia controlled the tempo. They controlled the paint. They controlled Steve and the scoreboard. Before halftime, we were trail-ing 42–33. No one was happy about it, but no one was unhappier than Steve. He was our strongest player, but he always put the team ahead of himself, which earned him credibility and trust. So when Steve stood up in the dressing room at halftime and started calling out his teammates—that we weren't screening hard enough, that we weren't fighting for position in the paint aggressively enough, that we weren't leaving it all out there—it wasn't the best player rag-ging on the rest of the team. It was a brother wanting the best from his brothers. He was challenging them. Character is built over time and in layers, like lacquer on a floor. Everyone sees the shine, but you're only as good as the hardwood underneath and all the polish that has come before the finished product.

The right message from the right player at the right time is the best coaching you can have; there wasn't much left for me to say. I reminded the guys why we were there, that this was their chance to show their country that they could do the impossible. They were all ears.

We got back into the game, and Steve took over. He hit a three off the top and played like a man possessed for the next twenty minutes. He even got into it with Yugoslavia's point guard, Dragan Lukovski.

There were so many TV time-outs that I was running out of instructions and inspiration. Late in the game, while we were on defence, one more break was announced, and the guys gathered around me at the bench. It was a crucial possession.

"I have fifty dollars for whoever comes up with this rebound," I said. They took to the floor, and I swear there were ten hands clawing for that ball at the next shot. A reflection of funding levels for sport in Canada?

Guarasci came down with the ball and handed it over to Nash, and as he ran up the floor, he yelled, "The fifty dollars is mine!"

Steve was so locked in at one point that he hit a three to tie the score, watched Dragan hit one immediately after, and then ran the ball right back at him to hit a three and put us up 71–69. It was our first lead since the game was a minute old, and there were only six minutes left on the clock. We kept piling on, and I gave less and less direction the closer we got to the end of the game; sometimes the best way to coach is to stay out of the way. Whatever it took to win, we did, and when the final buzzer went, it was Canada 83, Yugoslavia 75. We'd ended the run of the heartbreaking, medal-stealing Yugoslavia wins against Canada that had gone on since 1983 in Edmonton, and we'd proved to all the naysayers that we didn't need a tiebreaker.

In my mind, it was one of the greatest wins in Canadian basketball history, and much of the credit went to Steve. He'd scored or assisted on 18 of our last 21 points.

"That was like watching the Paul Henderson of basketball play," Todd MacCulloch said.

We were first in our group, which meant we would avoid playing the Americans in the quarterfinals. We were just one win away from the medal round. When I walked into the dressing room, the guys were going crazy. They were so happy, and they deserved to be. I remembered feeling the exact same way after our big wins a decade earlier. But as a coach, I couldn't let them get caught up in the win. My job was to tell them what was lurking around the corner. I didn't want to interrupt and make a big speech, so I just wrote one word on the whiteboard: France.

For the first time in the tournament, Canada was the favourite on paper as France had finished fourth in its pool.

"Our focus this summer has always been on the process," I told the team. "Making sure we've covered everything we can so that when it comes time to play, we can be satisfied with our effort, whatever the outcome."

There was no denying that we had come a long way from Puerto Rico the year before. Then, we couldn't get a single Canadian journalist to cover us during the qualifiers. Now, if we won the next game, we would have two cracks at a medal. Suddenly, we were the "it" story for Canada at the Games.

I reminded the team that unless they could harness their emotions as fuel for their performance, they would have to steel themselves for battle. I didn't want them to think past the next game to the possibility of Canada's first basketball medal since 1936. If they got too caught up looking ahead, they'd never be able to execute the game in front of them. And I especially didn't want them to think about what it would mean if this was the end of the tournament for them. If they did, they would only be selling themselves short.

France was a tough, athletic team, and it had the advantage of having watched us play five games. By then the scouting report was plain: the best way to kill a snake is to cut off its head, and Steve was the head of our snake. I knew that it would likely come down to what kind of refereeing we got. If it was a tight whistle and Steve could move freely, we'd be fine.

We followed all our rituals. We had our meal four hours before tip-off. We had our meeting to go through our scouting reports. We all lined up and touched the Canadian flag that Jon Lee hung beside the door for every game. And then we tried to make history.

As predicted, France made a point of muscling Steve on and off the ball right from the whistle. What we hadn't predicted, though, was that Makan Dioumassi, a six-foot-five guard, would be playing. The team had added him to its roster the year before in case it needed a defensive stopper, but he hadn't played much in the tournament. Until now. He played thirty minutes, every one of them against Steve.

At halftime, we were down by 15 points. Apart from a brief run in the second half that cut the lead to 6, we never got control of the game. Dioumassi was a big part of that. He shoved, grabbed, and knocked Steve down, and the refs barely blew their whistle, but that's international basketball. A different type of refereeing, a different game, and Steve would have been shooting fifteen free throws and the French opponents would have been getting fouls. Instead, Steve ended up making nine turnovers and was completely off his game.

We lost 68–63. As the clock ran out, Steve began to sob, huge body-shaking gasps. The game had been close, but "close" meant our dreams of a medal were out of reach. Sherman and I carried Steve off the floor and into the dressing room.

I went over everything in my head, wondering if there was anything we could have done differently, but in the end, you dance with whoever brought you. France was on a roll that took it all the way to the silver medal in their first Olympic appearance since 1984.

I looked around at the tearful faces of my players in the locker room. There was no way to explain the disappointment. Guys sat in their stalls, staring blankly at the floor or running their hands through their hair. We all knew that our quest for a medal was over, but there was still another game to play. We were so drained, though, that it was hard to stay motivated. I tried to put things into perspective.

"I am incredibly proud of you all," I said. "You believed in yourselves, and you came further than anyone thought you could. You've made Canada proud."

I couldn't help but think about Terry Fox. He had never reached his goal, but no one would ever call him a failure. In our own way, we'd done the same. No one had thought we could even qualify for the Olympics, but we had, and we'd almost made it to the medal round. That's not failing. That's living. We opened eyes to the future of Canadian basketball, and despite the clouds that day, I thought the future looked very bright.

CHAPTER 9

ENTERING THE NBA

The period after the Olympics heading into the 2000–01 NBA season left me in a state of limbo. There is always a bit of letdown after the Olympics, but this wasn't what I had experienced as a player. I had a job, three kids—now six, eight, and ten, and all busy with school and sports—and plenty of things to get a move on with once I got back from Sydney. The problem? The Grizzlies, it was becoming clear, weren't destined to stay in Vancouver much longer, which meant that my days with the NBA were limited. Rumours swirled about the club moving to a new location.

In September 1999, it was announced that the club had been sold to St. Louis Blues owner Bill Laurie, whose goal was to move the club to St. Louis—he even had a relocation bonus in the contract that would have paid the existing owner, John McCaw, Jr., an extra $52 million if the franchise moved. In the end, that deal didn't go through, but the writing was on the wall. The team was more valuable if it wasn't in Vancouver. When the team finally did sell, it was to an American businessman, Michael Heisley. When he bought the franchise in 2000, Heisley said the goal was to keep the team in Vancouver. But by March 2001, he decided to move the team to Memphis, Tennessee.

For me, that was a problem. Much of the team's staff could relocate along with the club. But there were two roles that very obviously wouldn't travel well: colour analyst—a role that I had gotten in part because I was identifiable to a BC basketball audience—and community relations officer. One of the first hires the owner would make in a new city would be someone familiar with the community in that particular market, and I was not going to be that guy in Memphis. So I was poised to be out of a job—two, actually.

But I had a bigger problem. My two years of coaching the national team and my experience in Sydney had confirmed what I'd known for a while now—what I really wanted to do was coach full-time. I realized that broadcasting wasn't going to be enough to satisfy my competitive nature, and my experiences in Sydney had given me a ton of confidence.

In the meantime, though, I had to make a living. The first opportunity that came my way after the Grizzlies left was as an AM radio host on a morning sports talk show. It wasn't something I'd ever pictured myself doing, but it seemed as though it could be fun. My host was Bill Courage, a good friend, so that helped. But you never know what you're getting yourself into.

My first day at work was September 11, 2001. I was doing the morning show in Vancouver, and we went on the air at 6 a.m. Forty minutes into my first broadcast, it looked as though World War III were breaking out.

"Is this real?" one caller asked.

"It's real," I said. "You're on air."

"Holy shit."

We were hoping it was some kind of hoax or practical joke, but it quickly became clear that something catastrophic had happened. In the moment, it was impossible to understand the context of it. We lasted only an hour on the show that day; once the gravity of the whole thing was understood, the station had to pull us off.

"You guys are off the air," our producer said. "We're going all news. We've got to broadcast this." It was a hell of a first day at work.

My gig at the radio station didn't last long after that. It was impossible to stay away from basketball. Canada Basketball didn't have the resources to make the national coach into a full-time role—the team just wasn't busy enough in the winters to justify it. I would have to look elsewhere if I was going to stay connected to the game I loved.

Luckily, there was still hope for Canadian basketball. At the same time that the Grizzlies were fading, the Raptors were starting to take off in Toronto—proof of what might have been had the Grizzlies drafted an all-star-calibre player such as Vince Carter. The Raptors' television ratings were beginning to pop, and the team was gaining popularity. In December 2001, TSN contacted me about commuting to Toronto to be part of its broadcast panel.

Younger Canadian coaches ask me all the time about how I got into the NBA and—by extension—how they could follow in my footsteps. Fair question. Many coaches have the skills to contribute to an NBA staff. The trick is getting your foot in the door, and unfortunately there is no magic formula to make that happen. It's about being the best coach you can possibly be, being a good person, someone whom people want to go to bat for, and then, frankly, you need to get lucky.

Early into my time on the broadcast panel, things took another turn. On December 23, Stan Albeck, one of the Raptors' assistant coaches, had a stroke about thirty minutes before the Raptors were about to tip off against the Miami Heat. Stan was one of the most respected assistant coaches in the NBA and Raptors head coach Lenny Wilkens's right-hand man, and he was supposed to give the players a pregame brief, when his face started turning red. He sat in a stall, unable to speak, while everyone started shouting for the team doctor.

I was glad to hear later that Stan recovered, but sadly, he would never coach again. A few days later, I stopped by the Raptors' morning shootaround—I often went to practices as a reporter to pick up stories. After the rest of the media left, I decided to take a chance and approached Lenny Wilkens.

"Lenny," I said, "if you need another coach on staff for the game, I'm happy to step in."

"Thanks, Jay," he said, clearly distracted. "I'll keep that in mind."

The team didn't call on me right away, but I think letting the organization know that I was willing to leave broadcasting for coaching planted a seed, because over the next few months, things started moving. The Raptors' general manager, Glen Grunwald, was also on the board of Canada Basketball, and our 5–2 record at the Olympics hadn't gone unnoticed. Early into the summer of 2002, I got a call from Glen.

"Jay, I'm wondering if you might be interested in joining the team in an official coaching capacity," he said.

The hair on the back of my neck stood up. *It's happening*, I thought. "Of course!" I said. "I'd be honoured."

"Nothing is certain yet," Glen continued. "I'll have to talk with Lenny. Keep your phone close to you."

I took Glen's words to heart, maybe a little too seriously. A few days later, my two oldest kids—Courtney and Jessica—and I went kayaking at a nearby beach. We stowed our clothes on our boats, and I wrapped my flip phone in my shirt, wanting to have it close by in case Glen called. We were playing around in the ocean, having fun, and in the midst of it all, I forgot I had my phone with me. When I climbed back into my kayak, my gear shifted and I watched helplessly as my phone splashed into the water, sinking to the bottom of the Pacific.

"Dad, was that your phone?" Jessi piped up.

"Aren't you waiting for a call?" Courtney asked.

Just the most important one of my career, I thought as I tried to stay calm.

"All right, you two," I said. "We need to get back to shore, double time."

We paddled back as fast as possible and raced home. I was so worried I'd missed Glen's call that I immediately dialed his number from our landline the moment we got through the door.

"Jay, I'm glad you called—I was just about to reach out," Glen said.

Looks like I dodged a bullet, I thought.

"I've set up a lunch with Lenny in Seattle for later this week. Can you make it?"

"No trouble at all," I said. "It'd be my pleasure."

As I drove down to Seattle later that week, I thought about when I'd first moved out west to start university. At that time, Lenny had been coaching the Seattle SuperSonics, and I couldn't count how many of his games I'd listened to on the radio while driving around the Pacific Northwest in my van.

Lenny was a legend, but he couldn't have been a less threatening guy. He didn't need to make you feel small or prove anything. He and I had lunch, and it felt like less of an interview and more of a conversation between friends. We chatted about the Raptors, the Olympics, and my work with the Grizzlies. I kept trying to talk strategy to show that I knew my stuff, but Lenny always steered us back to general basketball talk. At the end of it, he said, "I want you to work with us."

"I'd love that," I responded.

"Let me talk with Glen, and we'll get in touch soon."

I felt great on the drive back from Seattle to Vancouver. I couldn't predict anything for certain, but the thought that there was even a chance I could be coaching with an NBA team had me fired up.

A couple of days later, Glen called to officially offer me a job as an assistant coach. I couldn't believe it. I immediately agreed and shared the news with my family.

"It's going to be a big change," I told the kids. Thankfully, they were resilient and always found a positive.

"At least this means we'll be closer to Grandma and Grandpa," Dustin said.

•

Here's the thing: Being a head coach with the national team doesn't necessarily prepare you for coaching in the NBA. Nothing does. It's a completely different universe. Many people say that the hardest thing is to get into the NBA, and there's some truth to that. But staying in it might be the toughest trick of all. You're learning on the fly, and every move is being evaluated. The key to surviving is to have a mentor—someone who can show you the ropes and help keep you centred when things get tough.

I was lucky to have such a mentor in Craig Neal. Craig was one of Lenny's assistant coaches, and he had been around the block over the course of a long career. Craig had joined the Raptors a couple of years before I came on board, so maybe it was because he was new in the job and could remember his own transition, but he was really generous in helping me when I first joined the team. I watched carefully as he took charge in the drills and let his energy buoy everyone around him. I tried to absorb everything I saw and heard. I was determined not to repeat any mistakes I'd made during my earlier coaching career at Simon Fraser.

As an assistant coach, part of your job is to prepare game plans for upcoming opponents—we call them "scouts." Each of the assistants gets a couple of days to look ahead at the next opponent. A few weeks into my first season, we were on the road, heading for games in Detroit and Atlanta.

"What's your next scout for us?" Craig asked me.

"Atlanta," I said.

"The team has an off-night in Detroit tonight. Why don't you fly down to Atlanta and watch them play a game live?"

"How?"

"Just put it on a credit card, and we'll expense it. It would be better for you to see the game live and see what kind of play calls you can hear. You don't have to rush back for shootaround in Detroit tomorrow. Just make sure you're back for the game and that you have your notes ready for the next night in Atlanta."

I had no idea that level of scouting was possible. So I flew from Detroit to Atlanta and met our advance scout, Micah Nori, who helped familiarize me with the Hawks and the plays they were running. *This is invaluable*, I thought as I tried to absorb everything.

As a coach, you're expected to know your stuff. We're always learning, of course, but it's our job to have the right information and insights at the ready. Every coach does that. But what makes a great coach is conveying the information in a way that players will respect. The players are a very discerning audience. The veterans have been through hundreds of practices and games and heard every scouting report told every which way. You can't fool them, and if they sense hesitancy or a lack of confidence from a coach, their patience can run out fast. Most aren't too big on second chances, either.

When I flew back from Atlanta, I felt good. I'd written lengthy notes and rehearsed what I was going to say to the team. The next day, I handed out my scouting report to the players and then stood in the middle of the locker room with my notes in hand to deliver my report. *Keep it short, sweet, and to the point*, I reminded myself. Players' attention spans are limited, so you don't want to drown them with information. I went through my notes, highlighting the plays I felt Atlanta would run, and I saw the guys' heads around the room nodding. *I guess I'm getting through*, I thought.

After the meeting broke up, Craig pulled me over and said, "Ditch the paper next time."

"What do you mean? I just had the plays written out—I want to get it right."

"Can you memorize that?"

"I guess, but the cheat sheet makes it easier."

"Get rid of it. The players will not trust you if they don't think you know your stuff. Not only do you have to know it, you have to sell the fact that you know it. If you're looking down at a sheet all the time, it looks weak."

From that point on, I never again held a piece of paper on the floor. Never. Everything was memorized. Sometimes I'd write a little hint on my hands—something like "1-3" to remind myself that on the first play, they should watch out for the forward—just in case I got stuck. But I swore I'd always do the work beforehand to memorize my message and deliver it while looking into the players' eyes.

As coaches, we're used to feeling that we should have all the answers and the players are there to ask questions and absorb information. But they're the ones who are playing in the NBA, not me. At one point in that first season, my scout was the Orlando Magic. That year, Orlando had Patrick Ewing. It was his final season, so it wasn't vintage Pat, but we all knew he was destined for the Hall of Fame. I watched hours of tape, identifying Ewing's tendencies and coming up with a game plan, but I still felt I was missing something. A couple of days before practice, I went up to one of the Raptors players, Antonio Davis, who had matched up against Ewing a number of times throughout his career.

"I've got to present my scouting report tomorrow," I said to Antonio. "I've got Ewing—what can you tell me? I've watched about eight games of tape, but you've guarded him dozens of times, so I'm all ears."

Antonio laid it all out for me—Ewing's favourite moves, how he'd guarded him in the past, what was different now. It was smart, actionable advice, the sort of observations that only a player could make from the floor. I put Antonio's notes into my report, and the next night, we beat Orlando 106–97.

From that point on, I made a habit of getting the input of the players who actually had to implement the game plans I was creating. I recognized that I didn't have all of the answers, and that winning wasn't just a matter of drawing Xs and Os on a board—it was possible only if everyone on the court and off it was pulling together. I didn't know it at the time, but engaging Antonio was one of the smartest things I ever did in my career.

•

Little by little, I gained confidence and became more comfortable in the NBA. That first year in Toronto ended up being a fantastic experience in many ways. Sure, I was the fourth assistant and sitting behind the bench, but I was learning every day. Every day when I got home, I felt energized and upbeat—this was what I wanted to do. Even better, the kids were loving Toronto. They enjoyed their schools and were playing all kinds of sports. They had managed the move from Vancouver better than we could have expected. Things seemed as though they were unfolding perfectly.

But nothing can continue the same way forever, and the fundamental constant in the NBA is change. If you need certainty on a week-to-week, month-to-month, year-to-year basis, the NBA probably isn't the league for you. Players come and go; trades happen; management changes their mind or gets turned over. And coaches? When teams having losing seasons, they're often the first to go.

As much as I learned and grew personally during my first season with the Raptors, competitively, that 2002–03 season was a disaster. By that point, the Raptors were two seasons removed from their Vince Carter high point—the game seven loss to Philadelphia in the second round of the 2001 playoffs. Vince's injury issues were piling up, and we finished the season with a dismal record. But there wasn't any sympathy from up top, and that summer, Lenny was fired. His hall-of-fame coaching résumé was no match for a twenty-four-win season.

I had no idea where I stood. I had a contract, but that didn't mean very much—assistant coaches could easily be replaced. The most likely scenario was that the new coach would bring in a new staff and I'd be out on my ass. Beth and I had bought a house in Toronto when I was hired by Lenny, but after he was fired, Beth and the kids went back to Vancouver for the summer and we decided to register the kids for school there for the next year. I stayed in Toronto and kept working around the ACC, running draft workouts and making myself available for the players who were in town. The uncertainty weighed on my mind, but I still had my coaching duties with the national team, so I focused on those as I waited to see how things would play out.

Finally, in June 2003, the Raptors hired a new head coach, Kevin O'Neill. It wasn't immediately clear what role, if any, I'd have under Kevin. I tried to block out any negative thoughts and stay busy as the summer rolled along. I was still coaching the national team, and we often practiced at the ACC as we got ready for pre-Olympic qualifying. Kevin would pop his head in once in a while. I didn't think anything of it until he approached me in August.

"I've been watching you coach the national team," Kevin said. "The guys seem prepared and well organized. I can see you have their attention."

"I try to make sure I'm talking with the players, not just to them," I said.

"I can see that. I spoke with Antonio Davis—he says you work hard and ask the right questions. I need that on my team. How would you like to be one of our assistant coaches?"

"I'd love that!" I was thankful for the second chance, and I looked forward to what we'd be able to accomplish that year.

Flash forward to several months later. It was 3 a.m., and I was standing outside a Kinko's in downtown Minneapolis. A few short hours before, I had been in Toronto, watching my new boss crush diet sodas and coach his ass off against the Washington Wizards. We'd gotten the win, 82–79, in as boring and low scoring a basketball game as I'd ever seen at the Air Canada Centre. That was Kevin's MO: grind the game to dust and hope to be close enough to win at the end. It was ugly, but effective.

I had to make a presentation to KO and the rest of the coaches the next morning, and KO was a stickler for detail and presentation. For one thing, he demanded that all of the information be printed out on 11-by-17-inch card stock—he liked how the pages all fit evenly into his binder. Letter-size paper? Don't even think about it. Normal printer paper that you can get in the lobby of any hotel? Not good enough. Recipe cards? Nope. Which is why I was outside Kinko's at 3 a.m. in Minneapolis, hoping to get everything printed on card stock. I checked the opening hours on the front doors. *Of course*, I thought. *It doesn't open until six.* I headed back to the hotel to try to get a couple of hours of sleep, then it was back to Kinko's to get my basketball term paper printed out.

It was like that for eighty-two games. This was not Lenny Wilkens's world. Lenny had a great in-game feel that he'd gained from nearly twenty-five hundred games coaching and one thousand–plus as a Hall of Fame player. But he was not obsessive. We were once on the plane heading to a game, and Lenny turned to me, asking, "Jay, who are we playing next, after Atlanta tonight?" People talk about taking the season one game at a time; Lenny lived it.

KO was a different animal. He had worked his way up as a high school and small-college coach, then as an assistant with the New York Knicks and Detroit Pistons. He was a workaholic and just as demanding of those around him.

I appreciated KO's intense work ethic; I thought I knew what I was doing as a coach, but it turned out I still had a lot to learn. What KO expected from his staff helped shape the rest of my career. I learned how to draw plays on a computer, how to make personnel presentations that would stand up in business school, and how sticking to a system and a game plan could make all the difference.

Unfortunately, though, the season didn't go as planned, and after just one year, Kevin was fired as head coach. I was beginning to feel as though I were some kind of curse—first Lenny and now KO. Could I really be three times lucky and work for my third head coach in three years? Not only that, but Glen had been replaced as the team's general manager, too. Who would back me now?

•

At the same time that my professional career was in flux, my time with the national team was similarly chaotic. It didn't help that Canada Basketball was carrying a water pistol to a gunfight financially. We didn't have the budget to give our teams enough training time to build our depth. Figuring out how to run the program on a shoestring became a constant stress.

As I often did, I spoke with Jack about the challenges. "There are times it gets frustrating," he told me. "You'll never know the number of times I wanted to quit in the off-season. Then you get into camp and forget all about it."

I was grateful for Jack's wisdom and guidance, and I loved talking with him on the phone, discussing basketball or catching up on what was happening with our families. Jack's wife, Mary Jane, used to call me her "other son"—although with four girls and two boys of their own, I'm not sure they needed an extra one—so I knew we'd always be a part of each other's lives.

So I thought, at least. Jack was sick again, and things weren't getting better. Late in the 2002–03 season, I drove to Ottawa to visit him in person. We got to spend only a few hours together, as I had to drive back the same day for a team meeting the following morning. But seeing my old friend and mentor was always worth the trip.

Still, I wish we'd had more time together. A few weeks later, I got a call from Mary Jane.

"Jay, I just want you to know that Jack's time is coming."

I tried to hold in my tears as I digested the news. In my mind, Jack had always seemed indestructible—a force of nature and a permanent part of my life. The thought that we were about to lose him cut me deep.

"Thanks for letting me know," I said. "I wish I could be there with you all."

Jack died not long after. I was asked to speak at his funeral on behalf of the players Jack had coached. I spent a long time putting my thoughts on paper, trying to do justice to the man who had shaped so much of how I saw the world.

"I could talk about four consecutive Olympic qualifications and being ranked in the top six in the world for sixteen straight years. Or I could talk about winning the gold medal at the World University Games," I said. "But those are games and that is basketball. Those had to do with wins and losses. Coach was more than that."

I tried to keep my voice steady as I read the rest of my speech, talking about Jack's influence on all of the family, friends, and athletes in the room.

"Jack always said that success is about the journey, not the destination," I said as I rounded out my speech. "Coach, you have reached your destination. But the journey you created continues in all of us."

•

After we lost Jack, I turned back to the thing that had first brought us together and threw myself back into coaching. In the summer of 2003, we headed to Puerto Rico for Olympic qualifying. We had Steve Nash back but not Todd MacCulloch, whose foot issues, it turned out, were in part the result of a rare nerve disorder that ultimately proved to be career ending. It was a young team, with only six returnees from Sydney. There were four spots available for Athens, but the United States—because it hadn't automatically qualified by winning the World Championships the previous summer—was in the tournament and a strong bet to get one spot. Argentina was coming off a silver medal at the World Championships and was starting to become a powerhouse, with NBA stars including Manu Ginóbili and Luis Scola on their roster. We played them as well as we could in pool play, losing by four, but they handled us easily in the semifinals, meaning we had to play Puerto Rico in the third-place game. The winner would be heading to the Olympics.

There were echoes of 1999, when we'd had to beat Puerto Rico in the semis in San Juan to earn our Olympic berth. But these were different teams and a different time. It was our tenth game in eleven days, so I had been resting Steve and our other workhorses as much as I could, but we couldn't get to the finish line in front of ten thousand Puerto Rican fans who remembered what we had done to them a few years earlier. They were better than we were that night, and we were out of upsets. We lost the game and with it any chance of playing in the Olympics in Athens the next year.

As we headed back to Canada, it didn't feel like the end of an era, but looking back, that's exactly what it was. Steve and Rowan were aware that this might be the end of their careers for Canada. Having failed to qualify for the Olympics, our next significant competition wouldn't come until it was time to qualify for the 2006 Worlds. Steve would be thirty-four by then, Rowan thirty-five. Guys were getting married, starting families. Our window was already closing.

Failing to qualify hit me hard. When I fail, I fight back as hard as I can, and I struggled to find something positive in the experience. I had really believed that the 2004 Games represented our best chance at a medal, and now we weren't even going to be in the tournament. I resolved to do everything I could to get our young guys exposure to the best international play possible around the Olympics. If we weren't going to compete in Athens, I was at least going to make sure we were prepared for whatever followed. *We'll bounce back*, I thought.

In the fall of 2004, I was invited to lunch at the Westin Harbour Castle hotel in Toronto with Andrew Cook, Canada Basketball's manager of men's elite performance, and Fred Nykamp, Team Canada's new chief executive officer. It was only the second time I had ever met Fred. I didn't think much of being asked to lunch, but maybe I should have: it was a Monday, and Canada Basketball had just finished its annual general meeting. I was a bit late, as I was just running over from the Air Canada Centre after practice. We hadn't even looked at a menu when Fred let me know what lunch was really about.

"Jay, we want to make a change," he said.

"What do you have in mind?" I asked.

"We want you to resign as head coach," he said. "It was approved unanimously by the board of directors on the weekend."

I was stunned. I'd been so caught up in the Raptors' season that I hadn't thought for a moment that that was even a possibility.

"If you resign, it would make it easier for both sides," Fred said.

The organization wanted me to step down to avoid the appearance of conflict. Its story would be that I needed more time to be with my family and pursue my dream of being an NBA head coach.

My blood was rising, but I was able to keep my wits about me enough to tell them that their plan wasn't going to fly.

"No, I can't do that," I said. "I'm not going to quit on my players. That's all I ask of them—never quit. If you're telling me I can't coach, that's different, but I'm not walking away from these guys."

The meeting was over in a matter of minutes.

"Do you still want to order lunch, Jay?" they asked after everything had been spelled out.

I just laughed and walked away.

When the news hit, the organization went with the original story, saying that it hoped that relieving me of my national team duties would allow me to spend more time with my NBA job and my family.

"I appreciate them looking out for me" was my go-to line.

I hadn't seen the change coming. Coaching in the NBA was my job, but coaching Canada had always been my passion, and now it was no more.

The players didn't take it well, Steve in particular. When he was asked about it, he didn't hold back.

"We had a good thing going," Steve told Dave Feschuk of the *Toronto Star*. "The only failure we had was [losing to] Puerto Rico. . . . For us to get to that level, Jay overachieved as a coach, we overachieved as a team. It pisses me off."

After decades of being involved with the national team, I felt as though I'd lost a part of myself. I wanted to know more about why I'd been let go, but I was never one to dwell on adversity. If the team management didn't want me, fine—I would use that rejection as motivation to drive me forward. And if there was one thing I'd learned in my years of coaching by then, it was that when one door closes, another opens.

•

Free from my national team commitments, I found myself with more free time than I'd had since I was a teenager. That was fine, because coaching in the NBA was increasingly becoming a twelve-month gig, with predraft workouts, summer league games, and training with the players taking up a lot of the day-to-day. I figured I would take a break and head back west to join my family while I sorted out my next steps. Before I flew out, though, the Raptors' new coach, Sam Mitchell, called me in for a meeting.

"Jay, I was talking with Antonio Davis, and he said he's really enjoyed having you as a coach," he said. "I respect and trust my players' opinions. Will you stay on as an assistant coach?"

"Of course," I said. "I'm happy to help support the team however I can." *Thank you, Antonio!* I thought.

"I'm glad to hear it," Sam said. "I don't want you on the back bench anymore. I still want you to help develop our younger players, but I'll need your input during games more often."

I felt myself sit up a little straighter. "Of course, Sam. Whatever you need, I'm in."

As I left Sam's office, I thought back to when Jack had added me to the national team as his twelfth man. "You're a good guy and a good teammate," he'd said to me once in his typical blunt Jack way. "You make the most of whatever job you're given."

I was excited about the promotion, but it came with a learning curve. The head coach is accountable for every decision he makes. The relationship between him and the assistants can be delicate. The natural tendency is to agree with everything the head coach says or does—you want to support him and be seen as loyal. But the best assistant coaches are willing to respectfully disagree with their head coach and offer solutions, rather than simply point out problems.

Fortunately, Sam was open to ideas. "I'm not saying I'm going to use your ideas every time, so don't be upset if I don't," he told us. "But I want to hear them."

Sam's strength was his ability to relate to players and be honest with them. He could connect with the role players because he'd been one, and he could connect with the European guys because he had played there before coming to the NBA. But he'd also played with all-stars such as Reggie Miller and Kevin Garnett, so he knew the responsibilities of being a franchise player. He had that rare talent—the ability to tell players what they needed to hear, even if they didn't want to hear it. The rest of us on the coaching staff brought our own specialties to the table: Jim Todd, who kept things in perspective; Alex English, the basketball Yoda, full of experience and wisdom; and me, the detail and organization expert.

After our first year of getting to know one another, we put together an amazing season in 2006–07. We went 47–35, which tied the franchise record and was a twenty-win improvement over the year before. During the season, it took me maybe three minutes to get to work. I didn't even have to go outside—out my door, down the elevator, across the walkway, and I was in the building and on the job, either in my office with my staff or on the practice court on the third floor. For me it was ideal. I could eat, sleep, and breathe basketball, with minimal distractions. I felt I was starting to come into my own as Sam and I began to really click.

Early into that season, we were playing the Clippers in Los Angeles, and we were still getting used to the many new faces on the team, including our point guard, TJ Ford. The game was tied with sixteen seconds left, and Sam called a time-out.

"What play do we run?" he asked, turning to us, his assistant coaches.

"I want to set a ball screen for TJ at the top and then have someone else come up beside the screen," Sam said.

"Why don't we just let TJ go?" I suggested. "Clear out and let him attack?"

It was kind of a bold thing to do. Those end-of-game situations are highly scrutinized. No matter what Sam did, it would be on him. If the play worked, he'd look good in the eyes of the players and the media. If it didn't, it would be on him, and he wouldn't have the option of saying "Triano told me to do it."

"If we just clear out, we can let TJ go," I said. "He's the fastest guy on the floor—they won't be able to double-team him. Let's take our chances."

Sam went for it; better yet, it worked perfectly. TJ beat his man, got into the lane, and put up a floater from about twelve feet out. The ball was still in the air when Sam said, "That's in."

It was, and we won the game. As an assistant coach, there aren't that many times when you can point to a moment when you directly impacted the outcome of a game. Your rewards are subtler than that—a quiet nod or pat on the back from the head coach after a game, or the satisfaction of seeing a player improve his shot over the course of a year. But for one game, one moment, it felt great to know that I had been able to make a difference.

The whole 2006–07 season was like that. There were so many high points, and we kept exceeding expectations. Sam was named coach of the year, which was incredibly gratifying for our whole staff. I had been with the Raptors for five years by that point, and for the first time, things actually felt stable.

The success didn't come without sacrifice, though. During the season, Beth and I had split up. She and the kids had been going back and forth between Vancouver and Toronto, and the lack of certainty year in and year out had been hard on us as a family. The kids loved Toronto and their schools and activities there, but with the kids getting older, I didn't want them to have to split their time between two cities anymore. So Beth and I decided that it would be better for us to separate.

I kept the separation to myself, for the most part. It was a difficult, emotional time, and I saw it as personal—there wasn't anyone I wanted to share that information with. Plus, the NBA is a bottom-line business, so I didn't want to make whatever personal issues I had known, in case it changed the perception of my work or commitment. I loved being in the league; it is a tough job and a lot more people want to be in the NBA than there are spots, so it's important to be at your best at all times.

It wasn't until my exit interview after our 2006–07 season that anyone on the team knew about what had happened. "I had no idea," said Bryan Colangelo, our general manager, when he heard that Beth and I had split.

"Yeah, it was a tough year in that respect," I said.

"I give you a lot of credit for not letting it affect your work. It couldn't have been easy."

It wasn't. I missed the kids every day, and it was hard being away from them for so long. Seeing them only on school breaks and holidays wasn't enough. That was the downside of coaching in the NBA: you had to go where the work was for as long as it was there, because you never knew how long it would last.

CHAPTER 10

COACH TRIANO

In the summer of 2007, I got a call from Jerry Colangelo. Jerry was Bryan's father, but he was also a basketball Hall of Famer, and that year, he was in charge of the USA Basketball program.

"Jay," Jerry said, "how would you like to help Team USA prepare for the 2010 World Championships?"

Talk about coming full circle. Here was a Canadian kid who had been raised in the game by an American being asked to help Team USA prepare for the highest levels of international basketball. I wanted nothing more than to work for Team Canada again, but in the absence of that, I was happy to have a chance to reconnect with the international game. My response was immediate.

"I'd love to," I said.

A few weeks later, I flew down to Las Vegas to meet with the rest of the coaches. It was so hot in the desert at that time of year, you could barely go outside. But inside the restaurant where we met, it was cool and dimly lit. Everywhere I looked, there was basketball royalty: Mike Krzyzewski, better known as "Coach K," the renowned head coach at Duke University; Jerry Colangelo; Jim Boeheim, the coach at Syracuse University; Mike D'Antoni, then the Phoenix Suns' head coach; PJ Carlesimo, who had just won an NBA championship as an assistant coach for the San Antonio Spurs; and Nate McMillan, the head coach of the Portland Trail Blazers. Looking around the table, I wondered, *What am I doing here?*

The others knew exactly why I was there. From their perspective, USA Basketball was in need of an update. The team had finished in third place at the previous World Championships in 2006. Gone was all the goodwill the original Dream Team had inspired in 1992. Each subsequent iteration of the US national team had seemed less interested in being part of the international basketball community than they did in lording over it. Their attitude was bad enough, but worse—the team wasn't working as well as it should have. It needed a new approach.

Instead of trying to win internationally by throwing out a bunch of talent and hoping it was enough, the organization recognized that it needed to get better at playing by the international rules and building true teams, rather than all-star rosters. Bryan had recommended me to Jerry as someone whose international expertise and experience could help translate the nuances of international basketball for NBA players. My official role was assistant coach on the US select team—a collection of young NBA players who would be brought in to gain experience at the international level and to scrimmage against the main team when needed. My secondary role was to help the US players realize how the rest of the world viewed them and what they weren't seeing when they looked at the rest of the world.

Toward the end of dinner, Mike turned to me. "Coach, what to do we need to know?"

Me being me, I had come prepared. My notes weren't printed out on 11-by-17-inch card stock from Kinko's, but I had collected what I thought were the ten main differences between the NBA game and the international game. I talked about moving screens and how big men rolled early; how the United States could play the ball off the rim; the physicality of the international game and how there were twenty-three fewer possessions in a forty-minute FIBA game than in a forty-eight-minute NBA game, so players couldn't afford to waste a few possessions trying to feel out whether they were shooting well that day.

And then it got real.

"Jay, what does the world think about us?" Mike asked.

I felt everyone's eyes boring into me. I started off tentatively. "You know, with so many star players, you can be viewed as playing selfishly at times," I said.

"What else?" Mike said.

"There seems to be an arrogance there. You kind of behave like you're above everyone," I said.

"And?"

I decided to risk it and be completely honest. "You're playing against guys from other countries who have spent their entire careers dreaming about representing their country and winning a gold medal at the Olympics. To them, that's the ultimate privilege. There are NBA champions crowned every year; there is a new NCAA champion every year. An Olympic gold medal or a world championship? That happens once every four years, and you don't take it seriously enough."

I looked around the table. Everyone was nodding. *They're not offended*, I realized. *They're thrilled.*

"This is great, Jay," Mike said. "This is exactly what our guys need to hear."

"I'm sorry if that seems blunt, but I know you want honesty. Feel free to pass along those thoughts."

"Actually, we want the team to hear it from you. Tomorrow morning, at our first session, I'm going to start off with a quick welcome and then hand it over to you so you can tell the players exactly what you told us here at dinner."

"Um, okay."

Walking back to my room that night, I kept thinking, *What did I just get myself into?* How was I going to tell players like LeBron James and Kobe Bryant and Dwyane Wade, "You play selfishly and arrogantly, and the rest of the world hates you?" I don't think I slept five minutes total that night. But when I was about to address the players in the morning—the core of the so-called Redeem Team that would go on to win gold in Beijing in 2008 while playing a beautiful, respectful blend of the NBA style and the international game—it was Jason Kidd, the veteran and team captain, who pulled me aside. I guess Mike must have told him what I was being asked to do.

"Don't hold back," Jason said. "We need to hear every word of it."

And so began one of the most rewarding experiences of my professional career. Watching Coach K work was inspirational. More than anything else, he had an ability to lead. It was clear that the players on Team USA had incredible talent, but Mike's ability to break down the barriers between them and bring the team together was second to none. I could hear echoes of Jack in the way Mike always had a story or an anecdote to share that seemed perfect for the moment or that helped the group recognize that they were stronger as a unit than as a collection of individuals.

I still remember one practice that Mike led in the buildup to the World Championships.

"Lamar, come up here," Mike began, pointing randomly at one of the guys around him. He poked Lamar Odom in the chest with his index finger. "Does that hurt?" he asked.

"No," Lamar said.

"Exactly. But I see that in games sometimes. When things go wrong, we point the finger. Pointing a finger is a sign of weakness in this world. You will never see one of my Duke players do it. Just remember, when you point a finger, another three are pointing back at you. Now, Lamar, try and do a push-up on one finger."

Lamar struggled to hold himself up on a single digit. "I can't."

"Exactly. Get up."

I could see where that was leading, but I also recognized how Mike was holding everyone's undivided attention. He had a room full of future Hall of Famers transfixed.

"This is weak," Mike said, holding up his index finger. "But we still point it at other people before ourselves. What I love about the game of basketball is that a team is made up of five people. And if you take all five and put them all together, they will always be more powerful than one."

Mike made a fist and punched Lamar. "Did that hurt?" he asked.

"Yeah," Lamar said, rubbing his chest.

"A lot more than that finger, right? Now make two fists and get on the ground and give me ten push-ups."

Lamar ripped them off, no problem.

"That's right," Mike said. "The game of basketball isn't about this—one finger, one individual. It's about this: a fist, five as one. So when we come together in a huddle, our fists are raised as one. Now bring it in."

By that time, the guys were pumped. They jumped out of their chairs and raced together into a single group in the middle of the room, whooping it up as though they'd just won gold. It was amazing.

Then Mike got all the guys in the room to say what they believed they needed to do as a team to win gold. Kevin Durant, Russell Westbrook, Steph Curry—each of them took turns saying what they felt had to happen for them to bring home a gold medal.

A few days later, Mike got up in front of the team again and started talking about his name.

"No one can pronounce it, and no one can spell it," he said. "But it's my name. Your name is the only thing you have that is yours and yours alone. You have to value it. Think about where we sign our names. On all the big things, right? When you get married, you sign your name. When you buy your house, you sign your name."

Mike held up a poster. "The other day I was so impressed with what you guys said—you hit on everything it takes to win," he said. "So I got your ideas typed up and laminated. Here it is."

He slapped the poster onto the table.

"Like I said," he continued, "I only put my name on things that are important to me. I want to put my name on this."

He pulled out a permanent marker and signed at the bottom of the page. Before Coach K even finished signing, all the players in the room had lined up to put their name on the contract that they themselves had written. It was brilliant, and it worked—the United States started a new run of success for its national program under Mike.

"Was Coach K all he's cracked up to be?" is a question I get all the time.

"More," is my answer. "All that and more."

•

When the 2008–09 NBA season started, I was brimming with ideas and hope for the year. But it quickly became apparent that we would be fighting an uphill battle. We just couldn't seem to re-peat our success from the previous year. We made it to the playoffs again, but we regressed a bit. In the postseason we were beaten eas-ily in the first round by the Orlando Magic in a five-game series that felt more like a sweep. At the start of the season, you could feel the tension building. Bryan was a hard-driving boss—whenever things were going a little sideways, he wanted to see if we, as coaches, could correct it. A few weeks into the season, he travelled with us on a road swing. That's never a great sign when a team is struggling, and nothing went right in any of our games.

At our coaches' meeting on the final morning of the trip, we could tell something was up. Sam had massive bags under his eyes. He normally had lots of energy and was talking up a storm, but that day, he was quiet and so were we. Coaching staffs are like a team unto themselves. We work so hard and so long together that we can read each other's minds half the time. This time, though, Sam was direct.

"Listen, guys, I was on the phone this morning—I'm probably going to get fired today," he said.

The words just hung there. We all knew what that meant: if Sam was gone, our jobs were on the line, too.

"Sam, that's crazy," I said. "We're going to turn it around."

"No, I've been talking to my agent, and it's coming down. All I want to tell you is that I appreciate everything you guys have done to help this team. Your loyalty has meant the world to me. But if they offer the head coach position to one of you guys—I don't know if they will, but if they do—I would like you to take it. Don't feel like you can't take the head coaching job because of your loyalty to me," Sam said. "Go finish what we've started."

I loved working for Sam. By that point, I was his number one assistant. I'd been with him the longest, and I felt we were a good combination. A couple of months earlier, there had been some question about whether Sam would be back for the season—the success we were having had drawn attention, and other teams were looking at him. At one point, Bryan pulled me aside to talk one-on-one about my future.

"We're not sure what's going to happen with Sam," Bryan said. "But we'd like to keep you on in some capacity, no matter who is coaching."

I was quiet for a moment. Then I replied, "I think that, if Sam goes, I'm going to go with him."

Bryan's eyebrows jumped up in surprise. "Really?" he said.

"Bryan, I don't want to be the Canadian who's coaching in Canada simply because he's Canadian." No one works as an assistant for a fourth straight head coach, and I didn't want it to look as though I were some kind of Canadian token, kept around by Canada's only NBA franchise because of my passport. In my mind, if Sam had to leave for another job, I would have gone with him.

"I don't keep you around just because you're a fucking Canadian," Bryan said. "If you weren't a good coach, I would have gotten rid of you."

It wasn't the most straightforward compliment I'd ever received from one of my bosses, but it meant a lot.

After Sam broke the news to us in our coaches' meeting, I thought back to my earlier conversation with Bryan. I was still reflecting on it about an hour later when there was a knock at my hotel room door. It was Bryan.

"We've fired Sam," Bryan said, confirming my fears.

"Thanks for letting me know," I said. I figured Bryan had come by just to deliver the news in person. But he continued. "I want you to take over as head coach for the rest of the year," he said.

I was speechless. Just like that, I was an NBA head coach, one of thirty in the world. A wave of excitement washed over me, only to be quickly replaced by the gravity of what I was stepping into. *Where do I start?*

Bryan could see the shock on my face. "We've got to talk about a contract," he said. "Do you have an agent?"

"No."

"That's fine—you don't need one. This is what I'm going to offer you: you'll get your salary, and then we'll just give you a certain amount on top of that to finish up the year as head coach."

I felt myself nodding. "Okay," I said.

"We need to have a meeting today at five o'clock to address the team for the first time. Focus on how we want to play moving forward."

"Okay," I said, my brain still trying to catch up and process everything that had happened.

"You and I have to talk a little bit about that. There are a few things we're doing that I don't like, so we need to be on the same page."

"Okay."

I'm not sure you're ever ready to be an NBA head coach. The jobs are so rare that it's impossible to be properly prepared. In a perfect world, I'd have an off-season to gather my thoughts and a training camp to implement them. But the world doesn't work that way. That morning, I had been on Sam's staff; that afternoon, I was the first Canadian head coach in NBA history.

I didn't have the most auspicious start to my career as a head coach. Two nights after Bryan promoted me, we got drilled by the Utah Jazz, putting me at 0–1 to start my career. It wasn't lost on me that the same game marked Jazz coach Jerry Sloan's 1,102nd win of his Hall of Fame career.

The rest of the season was a blur. We finished 33–49—not a great record, although we did finish by winning nine of our last thirteen games. After the season was over, I suppose I'd shown enough promise, because Bryan thought it was worth offering me a full-time contract. We'd just started the summer break, but I was already looking forward to training camp that fall.

How thin is the line between success and failure in the NBA? Much thinner than almost anyone who's not in the league can possibly realize. I was determined to make that year's training camp—my first as a head coach—as productive as possible to set the tone for the 2009–10 season. We had a promising roster full of young talent that year, including a rookie named DeMar DeRozan, and I wanted to make the most of it.

We happened to be in Vancouver that year, and as we drove

through the city to the arena, I smiled, thinking about how I'd come full circle back to the city where my pro basketball life had begun more than thirty years earlier.

I brought in my old national team friend David Cox as our sports psychologist. I'd worked with David at Simon Fraser, and I knew he would help the staff and players get inspired and start visualizing their success. Every moment of the camp was scripted, from the guest speakers to the video reviews to the on-court practices, and everything unfolded almost perfectly according to plan.

The last day of camp, Bryan approached me, shook my hand, and said, "This is the best training camp I've ever seen." I hoped it meant good things for the season to come.

Things started off a little rough, but we really hit our stride in mid-December. We rode a three-game winning streak into the All-Star break. We seemed poised to make a run at a playoff spot after missing it for two years in a row.

Our first game after the All-Star break was against Memphis. Chris Bosh was exhausted. "I'm tired, man" was one of the first things he said after getting back. I understood—All-Star weekend is a good time, with a lot of events and not a lot of sleep. Players earn the right to be there, and I wasn't going to begrudge anyone their fun; it's a long season.

"Take practice off," I said to Chris. "But be ready to go tomorrow night—Memphis is tough."

The next night, we were up by 5 points with thirty-two seconds left. Memphis saved the ball from going out of bounds, and O. J. Mayo tossed in a three. *That's okay*, I thought, *we're up two, and we've got the ball*. But give a team a crack in this league, and they'll stampede through it. We tried to run down the clock, but then we missed a long two with eight seconds left. Memphis grabbed the rebound, sprinted up the floor, and nailed a layup at the buzzer for the tie. We lost all of our momentum, and Memphis ended up winning in overtime.

But the loss wasn't the worst part. Chris sprained his ankle badly in the extra period. As I walked down the hallway to the locker room, I wondered how we'd gone from being up five with thirty-two seconds left to dropping the game in overtime and losing our best player in the process. After that our season started to slide, and it seemed that nothing I did could stop it. Chris returned after a week, only to go down with another injury. We went on a losing skid and found ourselves fighting for a playoff spot. It came down to our last game of the season—if we beat Chicago, we were in. But our last-ditch efforts fell flat as we lost a close game at home. How thin is the margin of error in the NBA? A sprained ankle in an overtime that you shouldn't have found yourself in.

That summer, Chris left the Raptors for Miami as a free agent. It was clear at that point that the team was headed for a rebuild. No one speaks about it, but you can see it at training camp. Suddenly everyone's focus was on the young guys. DeMar was the focal point of the organization—the next up-and-comer the team would build around—and he was only in his second season. We had drafted Ed Davis thirteenth overall and traded for James Johnson, who was only in his second year. With such an emphasis on player development, the players knew what was going on. They always figure it out first.

As a coach, my goal was still to win every game and get the team to compete as hard as possible every single night. We'd had a great camp in Vancouver. I recognized that we had a young team, so I focused on the fundamentals, breaking down each and every drill to hone their skills and improve their basketball IQ. If we were going to build a new future on these young guys, I wanted to make sure that foundation was rock solid.

Things seemed promising to start, as we blew out Steve and the Suns in one of our first exhibition games. That might have been the high point of the season, though. The losses quickly started piling up. I wouldn't wish a twenty-two-win season on anyone, even if you know it's part of a rebuilding plan. My goal for myself for the season had nothing to do with wins or losses; it was all about helping the players I had and maintaining a consistency that they could rely on. I wrote it on the inside of the folder I carried everywhere: "Help these players get better. Stay positive."

I often found myself thinking of Rudyard Kipling's poem "If." My mother had given me a copy of it on a poster that I'd hung in my room in high school. I'd memorized the poem and have never forgotten it. More than once during that season, I repeated the opening lines to myself as a reminder that when you're confronted with difficulty, the best thing you can do is continue to have faith in yourself and keep your chin up.

The losing was tougher for my family than it was for me. They watched every game and heard every criticism. They understood basketball well enough to recognize the situation I was in. They were the ones yelling at the TV when things didn't go right.

My mom said it was harder watching me coach than it had ever been watching me play.

"When you played," she said during one of our phone calls, "I always believed you could do something to change the game. When you're coaching, it's like your job is on the line every night and there isn't anything you can do about it."

Mom knew what she was talking about, it turned out.

Despite our record, I badly wanted to come back and coach for another year. Who wants to raise kids for two years and then put them up for adoption? I believed I had done everything I'd been asked to do. I'd developed our young players. I had tried to keep things professional in a difficult environment. I had approached the whole year the same way: plan for the future and dream for it, but recognize that you've got a chance to make a mark today, so seize your opportunity. It was something I'd learned from Jack years before.

Late in the season, I was sitting in the coach's office with my assistants. We all knew that there was a good chance I would be fired and that, as a consequence, they likely would, too. The atmosphere wasn't great, to say the least.

"Guys, there's nothing we can do about this but our jobs," I said. "We still have a few games left, so let's go out there, be prepared, and never stop working."

When the season ended, I took the long walk up to Bryan's office for my exit interview.

"I'm impressed by the feedback the players are giving us," Bryan said. DeMar and some of the other players had come out publicly in support of me, which I appreciated more than I could describe. "We knew this year wouldn't be judged on wins and losses, and you've succeeded in all the ways that matter."

"I just want the best for these guys," I said. "I want them to be not just the best players but the best people they can be."

"I respect that," Bryan said. "But we're under a lot of pressure. I'm sorry to say it, Jay, but I'm afraid we're not picking up your contract option for next year."

I had seen the writing on the wall, but I was still crushed when I heard the words out loud. I breathed out deeply, trying to think of how to respond. Before I could say anything, Bryan jumped back in. "We still want you to be a part of the team," he said. "We'd like to offer you a one-year consulting position."

I considered the offer. It was unusual, to say the least. The new role would effectively make me a professional scout. It wasn't coaching, but at least it would keep me in the NBA. And the more I thought about it, the more it seemed as though I could do some good in the new position. There were plenty of talented young players out there looking for a break or a door to open, the same way I had before Jack had brought me onto the national team. If I could help some of those players find a home with the Raptors, I'd be doing something good. *Do the best you can today*, I thought.

A few months later, I was standing at the back of the press conference room at the ACC, watching Dwane Casey onstage as he was introduced as the new head coach of the Raptors. Casey and the team management laid out their plans for the team, their goals for the future, and how everything was going to be different. Afterward, Casey—one of the best people in the NBA—came up to me and said, "I don't know how you did it. All these young guys—how'd you set the course?"

I smiled and patted him on the back. "I'm not sure I know, either," I said. "The fun part is figuring it out."

CHAPTER 11

RETURN TO THE NATIONAL TEAM

I spent the summer of 2012 doing something I hadn't done in a long time: relaxing. My condo on Maple Leaf Square in downtown Toronto was quite literally across the street from the Rogers Centre. I could make it from my balcony to seats along the first baseline for a Jays game in ten minutes. That was my favourite way to relax, always has been—a beer, some sunshine, a ballpark, and my world was complete.

That summer, there was some sun, beer, and baseball, but basketball had—however briefly—stopped for me. My yearlong scouting contract with the Raptors was over, and I didn't know what I was going to do next. I didn't have an NBA job, and I wasn't involved in international basketball. I tried to savour the downtime, but in the back of my mind, I was constantly thinking *What am I going to do?* And then, in mid-August, my phone rang.

It was Terry Stotts on the other end. Terry was one of the most respected assistant coaches in the NBA. He had been the offensive coordinator for Rick Carlisle when the Dallas Mavericks had won the NBA title in 2011, and he had just been hired to be the head coach for the Portland Trail Blazers.

Terry had been my assistant coach one summer at a summer camp in Europe a few years before, and we'd gotten along great. We were about the same age, we were equally passionate about coaching, and we both enjoyed a good laugh. That day, though, Terry didn't waste much time on the phone. This wasn't a social call.

"I want you to be my lead assistant in Portland," he said.

"Sounds interesting," I said. "When do you want me to come out for an interview?"

"There is no interview. I'm offering you the job. You're the right guy for it."

"Are you serious?"

"Jay, I know you. We've coached together. I've seen you work. I want you for this job."

"Can I get back to you?"

"Sure, but I'm going on bike trip in a few days, so the sooner you get back to me, the better."

I had barely hung up the phone when it rang again. It was Masai Ujiri, then the general manger of the Denver Nuggets. I'd been out to Denver a few weeks before to interview for a job in the Nuggets' front office, and Masai was calling with an official offer. *It never rains but it pours*, I thought. Even then, Masai was recognized as one of the NBA's smartest executives, and I knew that working with him would have been fantastic. But it only took me a minute to realize that coaching was what I really wanted to do. It was in my blood.

In the previous year I'd spent scouting for the Raptors, I had taken the job incredibly seriously. I'd be up half the night at my apartment writing reports, and I took a lot of pride in the insight I presented about guys I'd seen who might be worth acquiring. But at the end of the night, I hadn't won or lost—I'd just sent in a good report. The players, the coaches, management—they all lived and died with what happened in each game. I missed that feeling.

I called Masai back and explained why I couldn't take the position he was offering. He understood completely. "You're a coach," he said. "Go coach."

I called Terry immediately after. "I'm in," I said.

"Amazing!" Terry said. "I can't wait to start working together again."

I couldn't, either. The only problem was that I didn't have a work visa. The Trail Blazers were working on it, but it was a complicated process, and we didn't have much time, with training camp just a few weeks away.

The solution was to have me participate in our meetings via Skype. I had my condo completely packed up in boxes and the moving company was on speed dial—everything was ready to go the minute my visa came through. In the meantime, each day, I sat staring at my computer, participating in meetings with my new coworkers, who could see only my head and an apartment full of boxes. When they wanted to show me something they were talking about on the whiteboard, video coordinator, Tim Grass, would lift the laptop off the conference table and point the camera at it. It was a little awkward, but it got us through.

I was looking forward to moving to Portland. Over my years

in the league, the city had always been one of my favourite places for road trips. I still had a soft spot for the West Coast, but the best part was that I would be close to my kids again. After my kids had moved back west, Portland had been the place where they could come and visit with me when I was on the road; there were no other cities within driving distance of Vancouver. On my off days, we'd go to the Nike campus store, which the kids loved, and wander the city, so there were a lot of fond memories for me there.

When I finally settled in, I realized how much I'd missed living in the Pacific time zone. On days when we weren't playing, I'd leave my office at the practice facility at 3:30 p.m. so I could be home at four and watch all of the East Coast games. Sometimes I was watching three games simultaneously across my computer, TV, and phone. Some days, at halftime, I'd hit happy hour at a local bar, get something to eat, and watch the second half surrounded by other fans. Then I'd be home by seven in time for the West Coast games. The best part? I was in bed every night by 10:30 p.m. The sleep deprivation I'd experienced in Toronto trying to keep up with all of the games and be prepared for my early morning meetings was a thing of the past.

Every day I went to work, I felt great—I was constantly smiling and bouncing around. "What's your secret?" people would ask me. It wasn't a secret or a mystery; I loved being in the NBA, I loved my job, and I loved the team I worked with. Portland was transforming me, helping me remember how I was happiest not when I was working as a coach but when I was living as one.

At times I did miss living across from the ACC and in the heart of downtown Toronto, where there had always been something going on. I could sneak into a hockey game or a concert and hide out unnoticed. In Portland, though, I was surprised to learn that the team went to the arena, the Rose Garden, only on game days.

"What do you mean—we don't go there every day?" I asked Terry.

"No."

"Is there an office there?"

"There's a table to work at, but you have to bring your computer and stuff in with you."

"Can we go to the arena and watch concerts?"

"Sure, if you buy a ticket."

It took some getting used to, but it wasn't long before I came to prefer the arrangement we had in Portland. The Trail Blazers spared no expense. Portland was one of the first teams in the NBA to open its own dedicated practice facility, and everything in it— the weight room, video room, therapy room—was first class. The players even had their own barbershop. What I loved most about it was that everyone in the building was invested 100 percent in the team. There weren't people there who also worked in sales or community relations. It was all basketball people, all the time. It was like being surrounded by family. You knew everyone in the building, and everyone there was invested in the same thing.

You could almost live at the facility. We had breakfast and lunch there most days, and there was always enough extra for us to take some food home with us. I never had groceries in my fridge.

"How do you live without groceries?" Dustin asked when he came to visit one weekend.

"They feed us at work."

"Where's your laundry?"

"I don't have any. I get changed at the arena, and they wash our stuff for us."

Dustin gave me a questioning look. "It sounds like you're kind of a kid again."

I was, and it made me want to go to work all day and into the night if needed. It helped that Terry was the kind of boss who made you want to dig in. He gave his assistants a lot of responsibility: creating game plans, running parts of practices. Our meetings were wide-open forums where anyone could say anything. Nothing was off limits. Honesty—even brutal honesty—was encouraged. The results of his strategy spoke for themselves: we won thirty-three games in my first year with the team—not quite good enough for a playoff spot but a sign of good things to come.

I loved the extra responsibility and having the chance to do more for the team. But just as important was what I wasn't doing. I don't think I fully realized the burden I'd been carrying as a head coach in Toronto until I started working in Portland as an assistant again. I didn't have to meet with the media three times a day on game days. Toronto was a very competitive media market, and people were constantly looking for angles and stories—it was just the nature of the beast, but it wasn't the same in a lot of other NBA cities, and it certainly wasn't something I had to deal with as an assistant coach in Portland. I could breathe again.

As a head coach, you're responsible for a lot of off-court duties— the job tends to be about a lot of things besides basketball. You're one of the faces of the team, so when the team is having an event for season-ticket holders or they want you to help with a sales pitch for a sponsor, you have to be there. I understood the rationale, but all I wanted to do was stay in the hotel and work with my assistants to prepare for our next game.

There were many times as a head coach when I'd be out for a two-hour dinner with the executives, and by the time we finished and I made it back to the ACC to meet with my assistants, they'd be on their way out.

"Coach, we're done, so we're going to go grab something to eat now," they'd say. "We're all set for tomorrow—everything you need is in the video and on the board."

"Thanks guys. Have a good night," I'd say as I headed back up to the office by myself.

Coaching is a brotherhood. It crosses language barriers, nationalities, and demographics. When you meet someone who identifies as a coach, who can whip up a bunch of ATOs—after-time-out sets—on a napkin at a moment's notice, who will go home after a practice and immediately start watching other games, you've found a kindred spirit. It doesn't matter what league or level or sport they coach. There aren't many people who can relate to the pressures and challenges we face, which is why getting together with other coaches, telling stories, and sharing knowledge isn't work—it's fun.

Being a head coach can be a lonely position, and I had missed the camaraderie of a staff and team. As an assistant, your only goal is to make everyone better. You're there to support your head coach and to help players get better. As a head coach, your only responsibility is to the team. Of course you want all the players to improve and reach their goals, and you set up your organization to make that happen. But you're not there to be the players' friend. You can't be.

The difference hit home for me when Ed Davis came to the Trail

Blazers as a free agent. I had coached Ed for his first two years as a pro after he was Toronto's first-round pick in 2010. In Portland, I worked with Ed almost every day, and as the weeks went by and we shared some laughs, we developed a great relationship.

One day, Ed stopped in the middle of our workout. "You're so fucking different now," he said.

"What do you mean?" I asked.

"You just seem like you've got a new perspective."

Ed was right. As a head coach, I had been so wrapped up in the starters that I hadn't had time to pay attention to a rookie who was just learning how to play in the NBA. That had been my assistant coaches' job. But now our relationship was completely different.

"Was I bad?" I asked. Ed had been around the league at that point—Portland was his fourth team. He'd been traded, a free agent, and now he was a vet.

"You weren't bad," he said. "You were just a young coach."

That, as much as anything, was what those years in Portland meant to me. I was able to focus on what I cared about most again— on basketball, on my players. I was working for a coach who was as significant a mentor to me as anyone had been since Jack, and for the first time, my coaching had nothing to do with Canada.

In my tenure with the Raptors, I'd always had the doubt in the back of my mind that my Canadian background was somehow the reason for my being kept around. I'd always felt that I had something to give to the team around me, but my experience in Portland was validation that I did bring value as a coach.

I felt as though I might have finally arrived at a point where I was comfortable in my own skin at the highest levels of the sport. But I wasn't content to simply rest on that feeling. It had been a winding road, and I'd been in the game long enough to know that I wasn't done learning yet.

.

By 2012, I was a different coach than I had been when I was let go by Canada Basketball eight years before. The organization itself was in a different place, too. Leo Rautins, my old teammate, had taken over from me as head coach, and the budget and personnel challenges he'd faced were familiar. Steve had never returned to play, and we'd failed to qualify for the 2008 and 2012 Olympics. We did make it to the Worlds in 2010 but went 0–5 and ended up twenty-second out of twenty-four teams. In fairness, that team had been missing some key figures due to injury, but even with everyone on board, it seemed clear that the NBA game was getting more international and Canada was falling behind.

But things were changing. Leo had stepped down in 2011 after we didn't qualify for London, and the program was at a crossroads just as our talent pool was finally beginning to deepen. Call it the Steve Nash effect or credit the influence of a generation of kids who grew up watching Vince Carter become a superstar, but it was clear that the pipeline of Canadian talent to the NBA was beginning to flow. Tristan Thompson became the highest Canadian NBA draft pick when he was taken fourth overall in 2011. His pal and teammate Cory Joseph was taken thirtieth. There hadn't been a Canadian taken in the first round since 2000, and there were more prospects on the horizon.

At the same time, Wayne Parrish, Canada Basketball's executive director and chief executive officer, had done tremendous work rebuilding the organization. Wayne was an excellent bridge builder, and since the day he had taken over in 2007, he'd made it his goal to reconnect important figures in the game with Canada Basketball.

Wayne and I had known each other for years, ever since he used to cover me as a player when he was working for the *Toronto Star*. He'd made it public that he wanted to bring Steve back to the program in some capacity. Over the winter after Leo stepped down, Wayne had reached out to me about his efforts to bring Steve in as the general manager of the senior men's team with Rowan as his assistant general manager. Wayne had also—almost casually—asked me about the possibility of my considering coaching again. By that time there was so much water under the bridge that it didn't seem like a crazy idea. There had been so much turnover in the organization that any of the people who I might have had an issue with—and vice versa—were long gone. I didn't think too much of it, but I said that I wouldn't rule anything out.

Not long after, I got a call from Steve. "Jay, Canada Basketball has offered me the GM's job with the senior men's team," he said.

"That's great!" I said. "If you need my support, my help on anything, you got it—you know that."

I meant it. After everything that Steve had done for me as a player, I could never say no to him. Our bond was twenty years strong at that point, and our competition had taken us all over the world. We'd had some of the best and worst times of our lives together.

"Jay, I told them I would only do it if you would come back as head coach."

I laughed. "Steve, that's a lot of pressure, man."

"Will you take the job?"

I paused for a moment, and I realized that this was the right kind of pressure, the good kind, the kind you feel when an opportunity has been presented to you and all you have to do is grab it and run with it. I was a different person than I had been when I'd first coached the national team in 1999. I was a vastly more experienced coach. My life was in a different place—the kids were grown up and pursuing their goals and dreams. My experience with USA Basketball had me bursting with ideas that I wanted to bring to the table were I to coach internationally again.

I thought about the younger version of myself in my earliest games with Jack as my coach, running up and down the bench with a clipboard in my hand, and how far I'd come since then. I could feel the familiar excitement coursing through my nerves, my fingers tingling, at the thought that there was a whole new generation of basketball players in Canada looking for the same opportunity to prove themselves and make their mark. I knew there was only one answer to Steve's question.

"If you're in, I'm in. Let's do it."

EPILOGUE

Of all Jack's lessons and unwritten rules, there's one that has stuck with me the most.

"Yesterday is a cancelled cheque," he'd say. "Tomorrow is a promissory note, today is cash in hand. The only one with any value is what you have in your hand. Don't worry about yesterday, and don't worry about tomorrow. Just make today the best day you can."

Those words gave me a lot of comfort through the years. I always kept his words close, but in 2016, I took things a step further. I had one of Jack's mantras—DREAM BIG DREAMS—tattooed on the inside of one of my arms. His wisdom about the value of the present moment was too big to fit on the opposite arm, so instead I went with NO DAY BUT TODAY—a tribute to my favourite song from the musical *Rent*. I figured Jack, who also loved the theatre, would appreciate the reference and the message about the importance of living each day without regret. When I put on a short-sleeved shirt for the first time afterward, I smiled—the only part of the messages visible was DREAM on one arm and TODAY on the other.

From the moment I started playing basketball, I've been dreaming. I've never stopped. So many of those dreams have come true. But there are a few out there still to chase.

In 2010, I was in Istanbul, Turkey, celebrating with the national team at centre court after winning the World Championships. Only, it wasn't the Canadian team I was with—it was the United States. I was finishing my tenure with the team, and it had ended on a high note as the Americans won the tournament for the first time in more than fifteen years.

I was happy for them, but as the team lifted me up to cut down a piece of the net, I couldn't help but think back to Edmonton in 1983, when my teammates and I had lifted Jack onto our shoulders to do the same after taking gold at the World University Games. That had been a triumph, the moment when we'd all realized that Jack's big dream, the one we all shared, was a possibility—that Canada could take its place at the top of the basketball world. *One day, Jack*, I thought.

I came crashing back to the present as I squeezed the piece of the net in my hand. I held it tight in my palm amidst the rest of the bedlam, as though I'd never let go. I knew the trophy wasn't mine alone. It was as much Jack's as it was mine.

On the flight back to Canada, it became clear what I needed to do. I had carried a piece of Jack everywhere I went for so long—it was time for me to bring something back for Jack, the American who'd brought a new basketball mind-set to Canada and led us on our quest. It was time to complete the circle.

I headed up to Ottawa shortly after returning. The Raptors' training camp—my first as an NBA head coach—wouldn't open for another week. When it did, I knew I'd be lost in the minute-by-minute grind of another NBA season. For those few hours, though, I thought of nothing other than going to visit my old friend. *No day but today*, I thought as I turned off the highway.

I was going to head to Jack's grave so that I could leave my piece of the net with him. But I decided to stop by his family's house first to surprise them. I knew that at Jack's family's home, I'd find the massive kitchen table around which we had shared countless meals, the backyard where we had spent countless summer nights talking basketball around the barbecue, the smiles of his family as we reminisced.

Everything was exactly as I'd thought it would be, and as I settled in to visit with Mary Jane and the rest of the family, it felt as though I'd never left. We caught up and shared memories, and then I showed them my piece of the net.

"I'd like to go to Jack's grave and leave it there," I said.

Mary Jane smiled. "I'm sure Jack would appreciate that, but why don't you let us keep it here so that it stays safe?"

I loved the idea. For Jack, teams were families and families were teams. There was no distinction.

As I drove home, a lifetime of experiences flashed through my mind: skinning my knees in my first tryout for the national team; tearing up after falling short in the Olympics; celebrating in the dressing room after defeating the United States for the first time. Every memory was a brick in the road that had brought me to this point. And every lesson from Jack was helping me pave the way for whoever would follow.

Jack's roots run deep. Ever since I started coaching in the NBA, I've encouraged the people I work with to share with one another: share knowledge, share passion, and, most important, share time together. That is pure Jack. His practices were meeting places. Basketball was something that brought people together. The court was a hub around which we all gathered.

Jack's dream was to do something great for Canada, for those of us who played and loved the game here. We wanted to win a world championship or an Olympic gold medal with him at the helm. That didn't happen, but he gave me so much more than a medal ever could.

The Canadian basketball family is stronger than ever. And there's one big dream we all share: to bring home a basketball medal for Canada. I want to take Canada back to the Olympics. I want our basketball team to stand on the podium and hear "O Canada" played and feel the weight of a medal around their necks. That was Jack's dream. It's still mine. It's the dream of many, and it lives on. I do believe it will happen. It might not be easy. But we won't stop. After all, we can all dream big dreams.

ACKNOWLEDGMENTS

When you coach, you inherit a little bit from everyone who's ever coached you. So many coaches helped me strive and reach for goals, fine-tuned different parts of my game, and taught me about the great game of basketball. In turn, those skills helped shape not just the player I was, but the person I have become, and for that, I'll be forever grateful.

Peter Higgins and Terry Boulton were my fundamental coaches in grade nine, Bob Erwin for a quick year in grade ten, and Paul Deeton for grades eleven, twelve, and thirteen at A.N. Myer. At Simon Fraser, it was Stan Stewardson and Mike McNeill, with Stu Graham always there as an assistant. Thank you all for setting me on my path.

Brian Mulligan was my personal coach who never stopped teaching me, and who continues to coach me to this day.

Jack Donohue along with Steve Konchalski and Donald "Doc" Ryan were my national team coaches. Thanks for the many incredible experiences and for giving me a chance to represent my country.

In the NBA, I've worked with too many assistants to name, but the head coaches were Lenny Wilkens, Kevin O'Neill, Sam Mitchell, Terry Stotts, Earl Watson, and James Borrego. For the US national team, I worked for Mike Krzyzewski. To all of them, I say a big thank-you.

Thank you to Michael Grange for taking this journey with me and for sharing your love of the game. I really appreciate your help in recapturing my thoughts and memories.

I'd also like to thank Sheri Parker, my everyday partner who has the rare qualities of having both emotional and educational intelligence, and who shares with me every endeavour I endure.

To my mom and dad, who taught me pretty much everything and allowed me to not have to get a job so that I could keep chasing my dream, I'm incredibly grateful for everything you've done for me. Thank you to my brother, Jeff, who competed with me in every game we ever made up, and to my sister, Jody, for having the best attitude about everything.

Finally, to my three kids, Courtney, Jessica, and Dustin, who had no choice except to go along for the ride. You've been so supportive, and along the way, I hope you've learned how to chase your own dreams and desires.